AF271686

Yours affection

George Müller

VALUABLE SELECTIONS FROM THE WRITINGS OF
GEORGE MÜLLER

GRANTED
MINISTRIES
— PRESS —

HANNIBAL, MISSOURI
WWW.GRANTEDMINISTRIES.ORG

TABLE OF CONTENTS

The great majority of this booklet was originally gathered and published by Paul Washer of the HeartCry Missionary Society, in volume 45 of their magazine (June-July 2005). We would encourage all who read this book and benefit from it to visit their website, *www.heartcrymissionary.com*. It is our hope that this booklet would increase the faith of all the saints.

TESTIMONY

Early Days

I was born at Kroppenstaedt, near Halberstadt, in the kingdom of Prussia, on September 27th, 1805. In January, 1810, my parents removed to Heimersleben, about four miles from Kroppenstaedt, where my father was appointed collector in the excise (*i.e.* taxes). As a warning to parents, I mention, that my father preferred me to my brother, which was very injurious to both of us. To me, as tending to produce in my mind a feeling of self-elevation; and to my brother, by creating in him a dislike both towards my father and me.

My father, who educated his children on worldly principles, gave us much money, considering our age; not in order that we might spend it, but, as he said, to accustom us to possess money without spending it. The result was, that it led me and my brother into many sins. For I repeatedly spent a part of the money in a childish way, and afterwards, when my father looked over my little treasure, I sought to deceive him in making up the accounts, either by not putting down all the money which he had given me, or by professing to have more money in hand than was the case, and counting it out accordingly before him. Now, though this deceit was found out at last, and I was punished, yet I remained the same. For before I was ten years old I repeatedly took of the government money which was entrusted to my father, and which he had to make up; till one day, as he had repeatedly missed money, he detected my theft, by depositing a counted sum in the room where I was, and leaving me to myself for a while. Being thus left alone, I took some of the money, and hid it under my foot in my shoe. When my father, after his return, missed the money, I was searched and my theft detected.

Though I was punished on this and other occasions, yet I do not remember that at any time when my sins were found out, it made any other impression upon me than to make me think how I might do the thing the next time more cleverly, so as not to be detected. Hence it came that this was not the last time that I was guilty of stealing.

At School

When I was between ten and eleven years of age, I was sent to Halberstadt, to the Cathedral Classical School, there to be prepared for the University; for my father's desire was, that I should become a clergyman; not, indeed, that thus I might serve God, but that I might have a comfortable living. My time was now spent in studying, reading novels, and indulging, though so young, in sinful practices. Thus it continued till I was fourteen years old, when my mother was suddenly removed. The night she was dying, I, not knowing of her illness, was playing at cards till two in the morning, and on the next day, being the Lord's day, I went with some of my companions in sin to a tavern, and then we went about the streets, half intoxicated.

Confirmation

The following day I attended, for the first time, the religious instruction, which I was to receive previous to my confirmation. This likewise was attended to in a careless manner; and when I returned to my lodgings, my father had arrived to fetch my brother and me home to our mother's funeral. This bereavement made no lasting impression on my mind. I grew worse and worse. Three or four days before I was confirmed (and thus admitted to partake of the Lord's supper), I was guilty of gross immorality; and the very day before my confirmation, when I was in the vestry with the clergyman to confess my sins (according to the usual practice), after a formal manner, I defrauded him, for I handed over to him only the twelfth part of the fee which my father had given me for him.

In this state of heart, without prayer, without true repentance, without faith, without knowledge of the plan of salvation, I was confirmed, and took the Lord's supper, on the Sunday after Easter, 1820. Yet I was not without some feeling about the solemnity of the thing, and I stayed at home in the afternoon and evening, whilst the other boys and girls, who had been confirmed with me, walked about in the fields. I also made resolutions to turn from those vices in which I was living, and to study more. But as I attempted the thing in my own strength, all soon came to nothing, and I still grew worse.

Six weeks after my confirmation I went for a fortnight to Brunswick, to a sister of my father, where I became attached to a young female, who was a Roman Catholic. My time till Midsummer, 1821, was spent partly in study, but in a great degree in playing the pianoforte and guitar, reading novels, frequenting taverns, forming resolutions to become different, yet breaking them almost as fast as they were made. My money was often spent on my sinful pleasures, through which I was now and then brought into trouble, so that once, to satisfy my hunger, I stole a piece of coarse bread, the allowance of a soldier who was quartered in the house where I lodged. What a bitter, bitter thing is the service of Satan, even in this world!

At Midsummer, 1821, my father obtained an appointment at Schoenebeck, near Magdeburg, and I embraced the opportunity of entreating him to remove me to the Cathedral Classical School of Magdeburg; for I thought, that, if I could but leave my companions in sin, and get out of certain snares, and be placed under other tutors, I should then live a different life. But as my dependence in this matter also was not upon God, I fell into a still worse state. My father consented, and I was allowed to leave Halberstadt, and to stay at

Heimersleben till Michaelmas. During this time I superintended, according to my father's wish, certain alterations which were to be made in his house there, for the sake of letting it profitably. Being thus quite my own master, I grew still more idle, and lived as much as before in all sorts of sin.

When Michaelmas came, I persuaded my father to leave me at Heimersleben till Easter, and to let me read the classics with Dr. Nagel, a clergyman living in the same place. As he was a very learned man, and also in the habit of having pupils under his care, and a friend of my father, my request was granted. I was now living on the premises belonging to my father, under little real control, and entrusted with a considerable sum of money, which I had to collect for my father. My habits soon led me to spend a considerable part of this money, giving receipts for different sums, yet leaving my father to suppose I had not received them.

Imprisoned

In November I went on a pleasure excursion to Magdeburg, where I spent six days in much sin; and though my absence from home had been found out by my father, before I returned from thence, yet I took all the money I could obtain and went to Brunswick, after I had, through a number of lies, obtained permission from my tutor. The reason of my going to Brunswick was, the attachment I had formed eighteen months previously to the young female residing there. I spent a week at Brunswick, in an expensive hotel. At the end of the week my money was expended. This, as well as the want of a passport, prevented my staying any longer in the hotel; but as I still wished to remain at Brunswick, I went to my uncle, the husband of my father's sister, and made some excuse for not having gone to him in the first instance. My uncle intimated, after a week, that he did not wish me to remain with him any longer.

I then went, without money, to another hotel, in a village near Brunswick, where I spent another week in an expensive way of living. At last, the owner of the hotel, suspecting that I had no money, asked for payment, and I was obliged to leave my best clothes as a security, and could scarcely thus escape from being arrested. I then walked about six miles, to Wolfenbuttel, went to an inn, and began again to live as if I had plenty of money. Here I stayed two days, looking out for an opportunity to run away; for I had now nothing remaining to leave as a pledge. But the window of my room was too high to allow of my escaping, by getting down at night. On the second or third morning I went quietly out of the yard, and then ran off; but being suspected and observed, and therefore seen to go off, I was immediately called after, and so had to return.

I now confessed my case, but found no mercy. I was arrested, and taken between two soldiers to a police officer. Being suspected by him to be a vagabond or thief, I was examined for about three hours, and then sent to gaol (*i.e.* prison). I now found myself, at the age of sixteen, an inmate of the same dwelling with thieves and murderers, and treated accordingly. My superior manners profited nothing. For though, as a particular favour, I received the first evening some meat with my bread, I had the next day the common allowance of the prisoners, very coarse bread and water, and for dinner vegetables, but no meat. My situation was most wretched. I was locked up in this place day and night, without permission to leave my cell. The dinner was such that on the first day I completely loathed it, and left it untouched. The second day I took a little, the third day all, and the fourth and following days I would fain have had more. On the second day I asked the keeper for a Bible, not to consider its blessed contents, but to pass away the time. However, I received none. Here then I was; no creature with me; no book, no work in my hands, and large iron rails before my narrow window.

During the second night I was awakened out of my sleep by the rattling of the bolts and keys. Three men came into my room. When I asked them in my fright what it meant, they laughed at me, continuing quietly to try the iron rails, to see whether I could escape. After a few days I found out that a thief was imprisoned next to me, and, as far as a thick wooden partition would allow of it, I conversed with him; and shortly after the governor of the prison allowed him, as a favour to me, to share my cell. We now passed away our time in relating our adventures, and I was by this time so wicked, that I was not satisfied with relating things of which I had been really guilty, but I even invented stories to show what a famous fellow I was. I waited in vain day after day to be liberated. After about ten or twelve days my fellow prisoner and I disagreed, and thus we two wretched beings, to increase our wretchedness, spent day after day without conversing together. I was in prison from December 18th, 1821, till January 12th, 1822, when the keeper came and told me to go with him to the police office.

Here I found that the Commissioner, before whom I had been tried, had first written to my uncle at Brunswick, and when he had written in reply, that it was better to acquaint my father with my conduct, the Commissioner had done so; and thus I was kept in prison till my father sent the money which was needed for my traveling expenses, to pay my debt in the inn, and for my maintenance in the prison. So ungrateful was I now, for certain little kindnesses shown to me by my fellow prisoner, that, although I had promised to call on his sister, to deliver a message from him, I omitted to do so; and so little had I been benefitted by this my chastisement, that, though I was going home to meet an angry father, only two hours after I had left the town where I had been imprisoned, I chose an avowedly wicked person as my traveling companion for a great part of my journey.

Outward Reformation

My father, who arrived two days after I had reached Heimersleben, after having severely beaten me, took me home to Schoenebeck, intending to keep me there till Easter, and then to send me to a classical school at Halle, that I might be under strict discipline and the continual instruction of a tutor. In the meantime I took pupils, whom I instructed in Latin, French, arithmetic, and German grammar. I now endeavoured, by diligence in study, to regain the favour of my father. My habits were, as to outward appearance, exemplary. I made progress in my own studies, benefitted my pupils, and was soon liked by everybody around me, and in a short time my father had forgotten all. But all this time I was in heart as bad as ever; for I was still in secret habitually guilty of great sins.

Easter came, and on account of my good behaviour, my diligence in study, and also because I was no expense to my father, but earned much more than I cost him, I easily persuaded him to let me stay at home till Michaelmas. But after that period he would not consent to my remaining any longer with him, and therefore I left home, pretending to go to Halle to be examined. But having a hearty dislike to the strict discipline of which I had heard, and knowing also that I should meet there young men attending the University with whom I was acquainted, enjoying all the liberty of German students, whilst I myself was still at school: for these and other reasons I went to Nordhausen, and had myself examined by the director of the gymnasium, to be received into that school. I then went home, but never told my father a word of all this deception, till the day before my departure, which obliged me to invent a whole chain of lies. He was then very angry; but, at last, through my entreaties and persuasion, he gave way and allowed me to go.

I continued at Nordhausen two years and six months, till Easter, 1825. During this time I studied with considerable diligence the Latin classics, French, history, my own language, etc.; but did little in Hebrew, Greek, or mathematics. I lived in the house of the director, and got, through my conduct, highly into his favour; so much so, that I was held up by him in the first class as an example to the rest, and he used to take me regularly with him in his walks, to converse with me in Latin. I used now to rise at four, winter and summer, and generally studied all the day, with little exception, till ten at night.

But whilst I was thus outwardly gaining the esteem of my fellow creatures, I did not care in the least about God, but lived secretly in much sin, in consequence of which I was taken ill, and for thirteen weeks confined to my room. During my illness I had no real sorrow of heart, yet being under certain natural impressions of religion, I read through Klopstock's works without weariness. I cared nothing about the Word of God. I had about three hundred books of my own, but no Bible. I practically set a far higher value upon the writings of Horace and Cicero, Voltaire and Moliere, than upon the volume of inspiration. Now and then I felt that I ought to become a different person, and I tried to amend my conduct, particularly when I went to the Lord's supper, as I used to do twice every year, with the other young men. The day previous to attending that ordinance, I used to refrain from certain things; and on the day itself I was serious, and also swore once or twice to God, with the emblem of the broken body in my mouth, to become better, thinking that for the oath's sake I should be induced to reform. But after one or two days were over I was as bad as before.

Sinful Ways

I had now grown so wicked, that I could habitually tell lies without blushing. And further to show how fearfully wicked I was, I will mention, out of many others, only one great sin, of which I was guilty, before I left this place. Through my dissipated life I had contracted debts, which I had no means of discharging; for my father could allow me only about as much as I needed for my regular maintenance. One day, after having received a sum of money from him, and having purposely shown it to some of my companions, I afterwards feigned that it was stolen, having myself by force injured the lock of my trunk, and having also designedly forced open my guitar case. I also feigned myself greatly frightened at what had happened, ran into the director's room with my coat off, and told him that my money was stolen. I was greatly pitied. Some friends also gave me now as much money as I pretended to have lost, and the circumstance afforded me a ground upon which to ask my creditors to wait longer. But this matter turned out bitterly; for the director, having ground to suspect me, though he could not prove anything, never fully restored me to his confidence.

As regards my own feeling, though I was very wicked, yet this desperate act of depravity was too much, even for my hardened conscience; for it never afterwards allowed me to feel easy in the presence of the director's wife, who, like a kind mother, had waited on me in my illness, and on whom I had now so willfully brought trouble. How long-suffering was God at this time, not to destroy me at once! And how merciful that He did not suffer me to be tried before the police, who easily would have detected that the whole was a fabrication! I was heartily glad for many reasons, but particularly on account of this latter circumstance, to be able soon after to exchange the school for the University.

Enters Halle University

I had now obtained what I had fondly looked forward to. I became a member of the University, and that with very honourable testimonials.

I had thus obtained permission to preach in the Lutheran Establishment, but I was as truly unhappy and as far from God as ever. I had made strong resolutions, now at last to change my course of life, for two reasons: first, because, without it, I thought no parish would choose me as their pastor; and secondly, that without a considerable knowledge of divinity I should never get a good living; as the obtaining of a valuable cure, in Prussia, generally depends upon the degree which the candidates for the ministry obtain in passing the examination. But the moment I entered Halle, the University town, all my resolutions came to nothing. Being now more than ever my own master, and without any control as long as I did not fight a duel, molest the people in the streets, etc., I renewed my profligate life afresh, though now a student of *divinity*. When my money was spent, I pawned my watch and a part of my linen and clothes, or borrowed in other ways. Yet in the midst of it all I had a desire to renounce this wretched life, for I had no enjoyment in it, and had sense enough left to see that the end one day or other would be miserable; for I should never get a living. But I had no sorrow of heart on account of offending God.

Friendship with Beta

One day when I was in a tavern with some of my wild fellow-students, I saw among them one of my former schoolfellows, named Beta, whom I formerly despised, because he was so quiet and serious. It now appeared well to me to choose him as my friend, thinking that if I could but have better companions, I should improve my own conduct.

This Beta was a backslider. When formerly he was so quiet at school, I have reason to believe it was because the Spirit of God was working on his heart; but now, having departed from the Lord, he tried to put off the ways of God more and more, and to enjoy the world, of which he had known but little before. *I* sought his friendship, because I thought it would lead me to a steady life; and *he* gladly formed an acquaintance with me, as he told me afterwards, because he thought it would bring him into more immoral company. Thus my poor foolish heart was again deceived. And yet, God, in His abundant mercy, made him after all, in a way which was never thought of by me, the instrument of doing me good, not merely for time, but for eternity.

About this period, June, 1825, I was again taken ill in consequence of my profligate and vicious life. My state of health would therefore no longer allow me to go on in the same course, but my desires were still unchanged. About the end of July I recovered. After this, my conduct was outwardly rather better; but this arose only from want of money. At the commencement of August, Beta and I, with two other students, drove about the country, for four days. All the money for this expensive pleasure had been obtained by pledging some of our remaining articles.

Trip to Switzerland

When we returned, instead of being truly sorry on account of this sin, we thought of fresh pleasures, and, as my love for traveling was stronger than ever, through what I had seen on this last journey, I proposed to my friends to set off for Switzerland. The obstacles in the way, the want of money, and the want of the passports, were removed by *me*. For, through forged letters from our parents, we procured passports; and through pledging all we could, particularly our books, we obtained as much money as we thought would be enough. Beta was one of the party.

On August 18th we left Halle. It will be enough to say that we went as far as Mount Rigi in Switzerland. Forty-three days we were, day after day, traveling, almost always on foot. I had now obtained the desire of my heart. I had seen Switzerland. But still I was far from being happy. The Lord most graciously preserved us from many calamitous circumstances, which, but for His gracious providence, might have overtaken us. But I did not see His hand at that time, as I have seen it since. Sickness of one or more of us, or separation from one another, which might have so easily befallen us, would have brought us, being so far from home, and having but just as much money as was absolutely needed, into a most miserable condition. I was on this journey like Judas; for, having the common purse, I was a thief. I so managed, that the journey cost me but two-thirds of what it cost my friends. Oh! How wicked was I now. At last all of us became tired of seeing even the most beautiful views; and whilst at first, after having seen certain places, I had been saying with Horace, at the end of the day, in my pagan heart, *"Vixi"* (I have lived), I was now glad to get home again.

September 29th we reached Halle, from whence each of us, for the remainder of the vacation, went to his father's house. I had now, by many lies, to satisfy my father concerning the traveling expenses, and succeeded in deceiving him. During the three weeks I stayed at home, I determined to live differently for the future. Once more the Lord showed me what resolutions come to, when made in man's strength. I was different for a few days; but when the vacation was over, and fresh students came, and, with them, fresh money, all was soon forgotten.

At this time Halle was frequented by 1,260 students, about 900 of whom studied divinity, all of which 900 were allowed to preach, although, I believe, not nine of them feared the Lord.

Conversion

The time was now come when God would have mercy upon me. His love had been set upon such a wretch as I was before the world was made. His love had sent His Son to bear punishment on account of my sins, and to fulfil the law which I had broken times without number. And now at a time when I was as careless about Him as ever, He sent His Spirit into my heart. I had no Bible, and had not read in it for years. I went to church but seldom; but, from custom, I took the Lord's supper twice a year. I had never heard the gospel preached up to the beginning of November, 1825. I had never met with a person who told me that he meant, by the help of God, to live according to the Holy Scriptures. In short, I had not the least idea that there were any persons really different from myself, except in degree.

One Saturday afternoon, about the middle of November, 1825, I had taken a walk with my friend Beta. On our return he said to me that he was in the habit of going on Saturday evenings to the house of a Christian, where there was a meeting. On further enquiry he told me that they read the Bible, sang, prayed, and read a printed sermon. No sooner had I heard this, than it was to me as if I had found something after which I had been seeking all my life long. I immediately wished to go with my friend, who was not at once willing to take me; for knowing me as an immoral young man, he thought I should not like this meeting. At last, however, he said he would call for me. I would here mention that Beta seems to have had conviction of sin, and probably also a degree of acquaintance with the Lord, when about fifteen years old. Afterwards, being in a cold and worldly state, he joined me in that sinful journey to Switzerland. On his return, however, being extremely miserable, and convinced of his guilt, he made a full confession of his sin to his father; and, whilst with him, sought the acquaintance of a Christian brother, named Richter. This Dr. Richter gave him, on his return to the University, a letter of introduction to a believing tradesman, of the name of Wagner. It was this brother in whose house the meeting was held.

We went together in the evening. As I did not know the manners of believers, and the joy they have in seeing poor sinners even in any measure caring about the things of God, I made an apology for coming. The kind answer of this dear brother I shall never forget. He said: "Come as often as you please; house and heart are open to you." We sat down and sang a hymn. Then brother Kayser, afterwards a Missionary in Africa in connection with the London Missionary Society, who was then living at Halle, fell on his knees, and asked a blessing on our meeting. This kneeling down made a deep impression upon me; for I had never either seen any one on his knees, nor had I ever prayed myself on my knees. He then read a chapter and a printed sermon; for no regular meetings for expounding the Scriptures were allowed in Prussia, except an ordained clergyman was present. At the close we sang another hymn, and then the master of the house prayed. Whilst he prayed, my feeling was something like this: I could not pray as well, though I am much more learned than this illiterate man. The whole made a deep impression on me. I was happy; though if I had been asked why I was happy, I could not have clearly explained it.

When we walked home, I said to Beta, "All we have seen on our journey to Switzerland, and all our former pleasures, are as nothing in comparison with this evening." Whether I fell on my knees when I returned home, I do not remember; but this I know, that I lay peaceful and happy in my bed. This shows that the Lord may begin His work in different ways. For I have not the least doubt that on that evening He began a work of grace in me, though I obtained joy without any deep sorrow of heart, and with scarcely any knowledge. That evening was the turning point in my life. The next day, and Monday, and once or twice besides, I went again to the house of this brother, where I read the Scriptures with him and another brother; for it was too long for me to wait till Saturday came again.

Now my life became very different, though all sins were not given up at once. My wicked companions were given up; the going to taverns was entirely discontinued; the habitual practice of telling falsehoods was no longer indulged in, but still a few times after this I spoke an untruth. At the time when this change took place, I was engaged in translating a novel out of French into German for the press, in order to obtain the means of gratifying my desire to see Paris. This plan about the journey was now given up, though I had not light enough to give up the work in which I was engaged, but finished it. The Lord, however, most remarkably put various obstacles in the way and did not allow me to sell the manuscript. At last, seeing that *the whole* was wrong, I determined never to sell it, and was enabled to abide by this determination. The manuscript was burnt.

I now no longer lived habitually in sin, though I was still often overcome, and sometimes even by open sins, though far less frequently than before, and not without sorrow of heart. I read the Scriptures, prayed often, loved the brethren, went to church from right motives, and stood on the side of Christ, though laughed at by my fellow students.

What all the exhortations and precepts of my father and others could not effect; what all my own resolutions could not bring about, even to renounce a life of sin and profligacy; I was enabled to do, constrained by the love of Jesus. The individual who desires to have his sins forgiven, must seek for it through the blood of Jesus. The individual who desires to get power over sin, must likewise seek it through the blood of Jesus.

– GEORGE MÜLLER

– II –

THE CONVICTIONS AND TEACHINGS OF GEORGE MÜLLER

These extracts from Müller's writings have been particularly used of God for the growth and benefit of many Christians.

On Faith

– A Common Faith (1842)

I desire that all the children of God, who may read these details, may thereby be led to increased and more simple confidence in God for everything which they may need under any circumstances, and that these many answers to prayer may encourage them to pray, particularly as regards the conversion of their friends and relatives, their own progress in grace and knowledge, the state of the saints whom they may know personally, the state of the Church of God at large, and the success of the preaching of the gospel. Especially I affectionately warn them against being led away by the device of Satan, to think that these things are peculiar to me, and cannot be enjoyed by all the children of God; for though, as has been stated before, every believer is not called upon to establish Orphan Houses, Charity Schools, etc., and trust in the Lord for means, yet all believers are called upon, in the simple confidence of faith, to cast all their burdens upon Him; to trust in Him for everything, and not only to make everything a subject of prayer, but to expect answers to their petitions which they have asked according to His will, and in the name of the Lord Jesus. — Think not, dear reader, that I have *the gift of faith*, that is, the gift of which we read in 1 Corinthians 12:9, and which is mentioned along with "the gifts of healing," "the working of miracles," "prophecy," and that on that account I am able to trust in the Lord....

From my inmost soul I do ascribe it to God alone that He has enabled me to trust in Him, and that He has not suffered my confidence in Him to fail. But I thought it needful to make these remarks, lest anyone should think that my depending upon God was a particular gift given to me, which other saints have no right to look for; or lest it should be thought that this my depending upon Him *had only to do with the obtaining of MONEY by prayer and faith.* By the grace of God I desire that my faith in God should extend towards EVERY thing, the smallest of my own temporal and spiritual concerns, and the smallest of the temporal and spiritual concerns of my family, towards the saints among whom I labour, the Church at large, everything that has to do with the temporal and spiritual prosperity of the Scriptural Knowledge

Institution, etc. Dear reader, do not think that I have attained in faith (and how much less in other respects!) to that degree to which I might and ought to attain.

Lastly, let not Satan deceive you in making you think that you could not have the same faith, but that it is only for persons who are situated as I am. When I lose such a thing as a key, I ask the Lord to direct me to it, and I look for an answer to my prayer; when a person with whom I have made an appointment does not come at the fixed time, and I begin to be inconvenienced by it, I ask the Lord to be pleased to hasten him to me, and I look for an answer; when I do not understand a passage of the Word of God, I lift up my heart to the Lord, that He would be pleased, by His holy Spirit, to instruct me, and I expect to be taught, though I do not fix the time when, and the manner how, it should be; when I am going to minister in the Word, I seek help from the Lord, and while I, in the consciousness of natural inability, as well as utter unworthiness, begin this His service, I am not cast down, but of good cheer, because I look for His assistance, and believe that He, for His dear Son's sake, will help me.

Oh! I beseech you, do not think me an extraordinary believer, having privileges above other of God's dear children, which they cannot have; nor look on my way of acting as something that would not do for other believers. Make but trial! Do but stand still in the hour of trial, and you will see the help of God, if you trust in Him. But there is so often a forsaking the ways of the Lord in the hour of trial, and thus the *food of faith*, the means whereby our faith may be increased, is lost.

–Strengthening Faith (1842)

This leads me to the following important point. You ask, "How may I, a true believer, have my faith strengthened?" The answer is this: *"Every good gift and every perfect gift is from above, and cometh down from the Father of lights, with whom is no variableness, neither shadow of turning" (James 1:17)*. As the increase of faith is a good gift, it must come from God, and therefore He ought to be asked for this blessing. The following means, however, ought to be used:

(1) The careful reading of the Word of God, combined with meditation on it. Through reading of the Word of God, and especially through meditation on the Word of God, the believer becomes more and more acquainted with the nature and character of God, and thus sees more and more, besides His holiness and justice, what a kind, loving, gracious, merciful, mighty, wise, and faithful Being He is, and, therefore, in poverty, affliction of body, bereavement in his family, difficulty in his service, want of a situation or employment, he will repose upon the *ability* of God to help him, because he has not only learned from His Word that He is of almighty power and infinite wisdom, but he has also seen instance upon instance in the Holy Scriptures in which His

almighty power and infinite wisdom have been actually exercised in helping and delivering His people; and he will repose upon the *willingness* of God to help him, because he has not only learned from the Scriptures what a kind, good, merciful, gracious, and faithful Being God is, but because he has also seen in the Word of God, how in a great variety of instances He has proved Himself to be so. And the consideration of this, if *God has become known to us through prayer and meditation on His own Word*, will lead us, in general at least, with a measure of confidence to rely upon Him: and thus meditation on the Word of God, will be one special means to strengthen our faith.

(2) As with reference to the growth of every grace of the Spirit, it is of the utmost importance that we seek to maintain an upright heart and a good conscience, and, therefore, do not knowingly and habitually indulge in those things which are contrary to the mind of God, so it is also particularly the case with reference to the growth in faith. How can I possibly continue to act in faith upon God, concerning anything, if I am habitually grieving Him, and seek to detract from the glory and honour of Him in whom I profess to trust, upon whom I profess to depend? All my confidence towards God, all my leaning upon Him in the hour of trial, will be gone, if I have a guilty conscience, and do not seek to put away this guilty conscience, but still continue to do things which are contrary to the mind of God. And if, in any particular instance, I cannot trust in God, because of the guilty conscience, then my faith is weakened by that instance of distrust; for faith with every fresh trial of it, either increases by trusting God, and thus getting help, or it decreases by not trusting Him; and then there is less and less power of looking simply and directly to Him, and a habit of self-dependence is begotten or encouraged. One or the other of these will always be the case in each particular instance. Either we trust in God, and in that case we neither trust in ourselves, nor in our fellow men, nor in circumstances, nor in anything besides; or we DO trust in one or more of these, and in that case do NOT trust in God.

(3) If we, indeed, desire our faith to be strengthened, we should not shrink from opportunities where our faith may be tried, and, therefore, through the trial, be strengthened. In our natural state we dislike dealing with God alone. Through our natural alienation from God we shrink from Him, and from eternal realities. This cleaves to us, more or less, even after our regeneration. Hence it is, that more or less, even as believers, we have the same shrinking from standing with God alone—from depending upon Him alone, from looking to Him alone—and yet this is the very position in which we ought to be, if we wish our faith to be strengthened. The more I am in a position to be tried in faith with reference to my body, my family, my service for the Lord, my business, etc., the more shall I have opportunity of seeing God's help and deliverance; and every fresh instance, in which He helps and delivers me, will tend towards the increase of my faith. On this account, therefore, the believer

should not shrink from situations, positions, circumstances, in which his faith may be tried; but should cheerfully embrace them as opportunities where he may see the hand of God stretched out on his behalf, to help and deliver him, and whereby he may thus have his faith strengthened.

(4) The last important point for the strengthening of our faith is, that we let God work for us, when the hour of the trial of our faith comes, and do not work a deliverance of our own. Wherever God has given faith, it is given, among other reasons, for the very purpose of being tried. Yea, however weak our faith may be, God will try it; only with this restriction, that as in every way He leads on gently, gradually, patiently, so also with reference to the trial of our faith. At first our faith will be tried very little in comparison with what it may be afterwards; for God never lays more upon us than He is willing to enable us to bear. Now when the trial of faith comes, we are naturally inclined to distrust God, and to trust rather in ourselves, or in our friends, or in circumstances. We will rather work a deliverance of our own somehow or other, than simply look to God and wait for His help. But if we do not patiently wait for God's help, if we work a deliverance of our own, then at the next trial of our faith it will be thus again, we shall be again inclined to deliver ourselves; and thus, with every fresh instance of that kind, our faith will decrease; whilst, on the contrary, were we to stand still, in order to see the salvation of God, to see His hand stretched out on our behalf, trusting in Him alone, then our faith would be increased, and, with every fresh case in which the hand of God is stretched out on our behalf in the hour of the trial of our faith, our faith would be increased yet more. Would the believer, therefore, have his faith strengthened, he must, especially, give time to God, who tries his faith in order to prove to His child, in the end, how willing He is to help and deliver him, the moment it is good for him.

–The Life of Faith (1855)
> *Reprinted from* The Autobiography of George Müller,
> *Whitaker House, 1984, pp.226-227.*

If anyone desires to live a life of faith and trust in God he must:

(1) Not merely *say* that he trusts in God but must *really do so*. Often individuals profess to trust in God, but they embrace every opportunity where they may directly or indirectly tell someone about their need. I do not say it is wrong to make known our financial situation, but it hardly displays trust in God to expose our needs for the sake of getting other people to help us. God will take us at our word. If we do trust in Him, we must be satisfied to stand with Him alone.

(2) The individual who desires to live this way must be content whether he is rich or poor. He must be willing to live in abundance or in poverty. He must be willing to leave this world without any possessions.

(3) He must be willing to take the money in God's way, not merely in large sums, but in small. Many times I have had a single shilling given to me. To have refused such tokens of Christian love would have been ungracious.

(4) He must be willing to live as the Lord's steward. If anyone does not give out of the blessings which the Lord gives to him, then the Lord, who influences the hearts of His children to give, would soon cause those channels to be dried up. My good income increased even more when I determined that, by God's help, His poor and His work would be helped by my money. From that time on, the Lord was pleased to entrust me with more.

–Faith Principles of Ministry (1834)

(1) We consider every believer bound, in one way or other, to help the cause of Christ, and we have scriptural warrant for expecting the Lord's blessing on our work of faith and labour of love; and although, according to Matthew 13:24-43, 2 Timothy 3:1-13, and many other passages, the world will not be converted before the coming of our Lord Jesus, still, while He tarries, all scriptural means should be employed for the ingathering of the elect of God.

(2) The Lord helping us, we do not mean to seek the patronage of the world; *i.e.*, we never intend to ask unconverted persons of rank or wealth to support this institution, because this, we consider, would be dishonorable to the Lord. "*In the name of our God we will set up our banners*" (Psalm 20:5). He alone shall be our patron, and if He helps us we will prosper; and if He is not on our side, we will not succeed.

(3) We do not mean to *ask* unbelievers for money (2 Corinthians 6:14-18); though we do not feel ourselves warranted to refuse their contributions, if they, of their own accord, should offer them (see Acts 28:2, 10).

(4) We reject altogether the help of unbelievers in managing or carrying on the affairs of the institution (see 2 Corinthians 6:14-18).

(5) We intend never to enlarge the field of labour by contracting debts (Romans 13:8), and afterward appealing to the Church of God for help, because this we consider to be opposed both to the letter and the spirit of the New Testament; but in secret prayer, God helping us, we shall carry the wants of the institution to the Lord, and act according to the means that God shall give.

(6) We do not mean to reckon the success of the institution by the amount of money given or the number of Bibles distributed, but by the Lord's blessing on the work (Zechariah 4:6); and we expect this, in the proportion in which He shall help us to wait upon Him in prayer.

(7) While we would avoid needless separation, we desire to go on simply according to Scripture, without compromising the truth; at the same time

thankfully receiving any instruction which experienced believers, after prayer, upon scriptural ground, may have to give us concerning the institution.

On the Kingdom and Its Treasures

—Seeking First the Kingdom (1844)

> *"But seek ye first the kingdom of God and His righteousness: and all these things shall be added unto you" (Matthew 5:33).*

After our Lord, in the previous verses, had been pointing His disciples to *"the fowls of the air,"* and *"the lilies of the field,"* in order that they should be without carefulness about the necessaries of life, He adds: *"Therefore take not thought* [literally, "be not anxious"] *saying, What shall we eat? or, What shall we drink? or, Wherewithal shall we be clothed? (for after all these things do the Gentiles seek) for your heavenly Father knoweth that ye have need of all these things."* Observe here particularly that we, the children of God, should be different from the nations of the earth, from those who have no Father in heaven, and who therefore make it their great business, their first anxious concern, what they shall eat, and what they shall drink, and wherewithal they shall be clothed. We, the children of God, should, as in every other respect, so in this particular also, be different from the world, and prove to the world that we believe that we have a Father in heaven, who knoweth that we have need of all these things. The fact that our almighty Father, who is full of infinite love to us His children, and who has proved to us His love in the gift of His only begotten Son, and His almighty power in raising Him from the dead, knows that we have need of these things, should remove all anxiety from our minds.

There is, however, one thing which we *ought* to attend to, with reference to our temporal necessities; it is mentioned in our verse: *"But seek ye first the kingdom of God and His righteousness."* The great business which the disciple of the Lord Jesus has to be concerned about (for this word was spoken to disciples, to professed believers) is, to seek the kingdom of God, *i.e.*, to seek, as I view it, after the external and internal prosperity of the Church of God. If, according to our ability, and according to the opportunity which the Lord gives us, we seek to win souls for the Lord Jesus, that appears to me to be seeking the *external prosperity* of the kingdom of God; and, if we, as members of the body of Christ, seek to benefit our fellow members in the body, helping them on in grace and truth, or caring for them in any way to their edification, that would be seeking the *internal prosperity* of the kingdom of God. But in connection with this we have also to *"seek ... His righteousness,"* which means (as it was spoken to disciples, to those who have a Father in heaven, and not to those who were without), to seek to be more and more like God, to seek to be inwardly conformed to the mind of God. If these two things are attended to (*and they imply also that we are not slothful in business*), then do we come under that precious promise: *"And all these things* [that is food, raiment, or any thing else that is needful for this present life] *shall be added unto you."* It is not for attending to these two things that we obtain the blessing, but in attending to them.

I now ask you, my dear reader, a few questions in all love, because I do seek your welfare, and I do not wish to put these questions to you, without putting them first to my own heart. Do you make it your primary business, your first great concern, to seek the kingdom of God and His righteousness? Are the things of God, the honour of His name, the welfare of His Church, the conversion of sinners, and the profit of your own soul, your chief aim? Or, does your business, or your family, or your own temporal concerns, in some shape or other *primarily* occupy your attention?...

I never knew a child of God who acted according to the above passage, in whose experience the Lord did not fulfill His word of promise, *"All these things shall be added unto you."*

–*Treasures in Heaven (1844)*

In Matthew 6:19-21, it is written: *"Lay not up for yourselves treasures upon earth, where moth and rust doth corrupt, and where thieves break through and steal, but lay up for yourselves treasures in heaven, where neither moth nor rust doth corrupt, and where thieves do not break through nor steal: for where your treasure is, there will your heart be also."* Observe, dear reader, the following points concerning this part of the divine testimony:

(1) It is the Lord Jesus, our Lord and Master, who speaks this as the lawgiver of His people. He who has infinite wisdom and unfathomable love to us, who therefore knows what is for our real welfare and happiness, and who cannot exact from us any requirement inconsistent with that love which led Him to lay down His life for us. Remembering then, who it is who speaks to us in these verses, let us consider them.

(2) His counsel, His affectionate entreaty, and His commandment to us His disciples is: *"Lay not up for yourselves treasures upon earth."* The meaning obviously is, that the disciples of the Lord Jesus, being strangers and pilgrims on earth, *i.e.*, neither belonging to the earth nor expecting to remain in it, *should not seek to increase their earthly possessions,* in whatever these possessions may consist. This is a word for poor believers as well as for rich believers....

(3) Our Lord says concerning the earth, that it is a place *"where moth and rust doth corrupt, and where thieves break through and steal."* All that is of the earth, and in any way connected with it, is subject to corruption, to change, to dissolution. There is no reality, or substance, in any thing else but in heavenly things. Often the careful amassing of earthly possessions ends in losing them

in a moment by fire, by robbery, by a change of mercantile concerns, by loss of work, etc.; but suppose all this were not the case, still, yet a little while, and thy soul shall be required of thee; or, yet a little while, and the Lord Jesus will return; and what profit shalt thou then have, dear reader, if thou hast carefully sought to increase thy earthly possessions? My brother, if there were one particle of real benefit to be derived from it, would not He, whose love to us has been proved to the utmost, have wished that you and I should have it? If, in the least degree, it could tend to the increase of our peace, or joy in the Holy Ghost, or heavenly-mindedness, He, who laid down His life for us, would have commanded us, to "LAY UP treasure upon earth."

(4) Our Lord does not merely bid us not to lay up treasure upon earth; if He had said no more, this commandment might be abused, and persons find in it an encouragement for their extravagant habits, their love of pleasure, and their habit of spending everything they have, or can obtain, *upon themselves.* It does not mean, then, as is the common phrase, that we should "live up to our income;" for, He adds: *"But lay up for yourselves treasures in heaven."* There is such a thing as laying up in heaven as truly as there is laying up on earth; if it were not so, our Lord would not have said so. Just as persons put one sum after another into the bank, and it is put down to their credit, and they may use the money afterwards: so truly the penny, the shilling, the pound, the hundred pounds, the ten thousand pounds, *given for the Lord's sake, and constrained by the love of Christ*, to poor brethren, or in any way spent in the work of God, He marks down in the book of remembrance, He considers as laid up in heaven. *The money is not lost, it is laid up in the bank of heaven*, yet so, that, whilst an earthly bank may break, or through earthly circumstances we may lose our earthly possessions, the money, thus secured in heaven, *cannot be lost*.

But this is by no means the only difference. I notice a few more points. Treasures laid up on earth bring along with them many cares; treasures laid up in heaven never give care. Treasures laid up on earth never can afford spiritual joy; treasures laid up in heaven bring along with them peace and joy in the Holy Ghost even now. Treasures laid up on earth, in a dying hour cannot afford peace and comfort, and when life is over, they are taken from us; treasures laid up in heaven draw forth thanksgiving, that we were permitted and counted worthy to serve the Lord with the means with which He was pleased to entrust us as stewards; and when this life is over we are not deprived of what was laid up there, but when we go to heaven we go to the place where our treasures are, and we shall find them there. Often we hear it said when a person has died: he died worth so much. But whatever be the phrases common in the world, it is certain that a person may die worth fifty thousand pounds sterling, as the world reckons, and yet that individual may not possess, in the sight of God, one thousand pounds sterling, because *he was not rich towards God*, he did not lay up treasures in heaven....

Dear reader, does your soul long to be rich towards God, to lay up treasures in heaven? The world passes away and the lust thereof! Yet a little while, and our stewardship will be taken from us. At present we have the opportunity of serving the Lord, with our time, our talents, our bodily strength, our gifts, and also with our property; but shortly this opportunity may cease. Oh! How shortly it may cease. Before ever this is read by anyone, I may have fallen asleep; and the very next day after you have read this, dear reader, you may fall asleep, and therefore, while we have opportunity, let us serve the Lord—I believe, and therefore I speak. My own soul is so fully assured of the wisdom and love of the Lord toward us His disciples as expressed in this Word, that by His grace I do most heartily set my seal to the preciousness of the command, and I do from my inmost soul not only desire not to lay up treasures upon earth, but, believing as I do what the Lord says, I do desire to have grace to lay up treasures in heaven.

(5) The Lord lastly adds: *"For where your treasure is, there will your heart be also."* Where should the heart of the disciple of the Lord Jesus be, but in heaven? Our calling is a heavenly calling; our inheritance is a heavenly inheritance; our citizenship is in heaven; but if we believers in the Lord Jesus lay up treasures on earth, the necessary result of it is, that our hearts will be upon earth; nay, the very fact of our doing so proves that they are there! Nor will it be otherwise, till there be a ceasing to lay up treasures upon earth. The believer who lays up treasures upon earth may, at first, not live openly in sin; he in a measure may yet bring some honour to the Lord in certain things; but the injurious tendencies of this habit will show themselves more and more, whilst the habit of laying up treasures in heaven would draw the heart more and more heavenward; would be continually strengthening his new, his divine nature, his spiritual faculties, because it would call his spiritual faculties into use, and thus they would be strengthened; and he would more and more, whilst yet in the body, have his heart in heaven, and set upon heavenly things; and thus the laying up treasures in heaven would bring along with it, even in this life, precious spiritual blessings as a reward of obedience.

On Stewardship

The child of God has been bought with the *"precious blood of the Christ,"* and is altogether His property, with all that he possesses: his bodily strength, his mental strength, his ability of every kind, his trade, business, art, profession, his property, etc.; for it is written: *"Ye are not your own; for ye are bought with a price"* (1 Corinthians 6:19, 20). The proceeds of our calling are therefore not our own in the sense of using them as our natural heart wishes us to do, whether to spend them on the gratification of our pride, or our love of pleasure, or sensual indulgences, or to lay by the money for ourselves or our children, or use it in any way as we *naturally* like; but we have to stand before our Lord and Master, whose *stewards* we are, to seek to ascertain His will, how He will have us use the proceeds of our calling. But is this indeed the spirit in which the children of God generally are engaged in their calling? It is but too well known that it is not the case! Can we then wonder at it, that even God's own dear children should so often be found greatly in difficulty with regard to their calling, and be found so often complaining about stagnation or competition in trade, and the difficulties of the times, though there have been given to them such precious promises as: "*Seek ye first the kingdom of God and His righteousness; and all these things shall be added unto you,*" or "*Let your conversation* [disposition or turn of mind] *be without covetousness; and be content with such things as ye have: for He hath said, 'I will never leave thee, nor forsake thee'*" (Hebrews 13:5)? Is it not obvious enough, that, when our Heavenly Father sees that we His children do, or would, use the proceeds of our calling, *as our natural mind* would desire, He either cannot at all entrust us with means, or will be obliged to decrease them? No wise and really affectionate mother will permit her infant to play with a razor, or with fire, however much the child may desire to have them; and so the love and wisdom of our Heavenly Father will not, cannot, entrust us with pecuniary means (*except it be in the way of chastisement, or to show us finally their utter vanity*), if He sees that we do not desire to possess them as stewards for Him, in order that we may spend them as He may point out to us by His Holy Spirit, through His Word.

In connection with this I give a few hints to the believing reader on three passages of the Word of God. In 1 Corinthians 16:2, we find it written to the brethren at Corinth, "*Upon the first day of the week let every one of you lay by him in store, as God has prospered him.*" A contribution for the poor saints in Judea was to be made, and the brethren at Corinth were exhorted to put by every Lord's day, according to the measure of success which the Lord had been pleased to grant them in their calling during the week. Now, ought not the saints in our day also to act according to this word? There is no passage in the Word of God telling us not to do so, and it is altogether in accordance with our pilgrim character, not only once or twice, or four times a year, to see how much we can afford to give to the poor saints, or to the work of God in any way, but to seek to settle it weekly....

It might also be said by a brother whose earnings are small, "Should *I* also give according to my earnings? They are already so small, that my wife can only with the greatest difficulty manage to make them sufficient for the family." My reply is: Have you ever considered, my brother, that the very reason why the Lord is obliged to let your earnings remain so small, may be the fact of your spending everything upon yourselves, and that, if He were to give you more, you would only use it to increase your own family comfort, instead of looking about to see who among the brethren are sick, or who have no work at all, that you might help them, or how you might assist the work of God at home and abroad? There is a great temptation for a brother whose earnings are small, to put off the responsibility of assisting the needy and sick saints, or helping on the work of God, and to lay it upon the few rich brethren and sisters with whom he is associated in fellowship, and thus rob his own soul!

It might be asked, "How much shall I give of my income? The tenth part, or the fifth part, or the third part, or one half, of more?" My reply is, God lays down no rule concerning this point. What we do we should do cheerfully and not of necessity. But if even Jacob, with the first dawning of spiritual light (Genesis 28:22), promised to God the tenth of all He should give to him, how much ought we believers in the Lord Jesus to do for Him? We, whose calling is a heavenly one, and who *know distinctly* that we are children of God and joint heirs with the Lord Jesus! Yet do all the children of God give even the *tenth* part of what the Lord gives them?...

In connection with 1 Corinthians 16:2, I would mention two other portions:

(1) "He which soweth sparingly shall reap also sparingly; and he which soweth bountifully shall reap also bountifully" (2 Corinthians 9:6). It is certain that we children of God are so abundantly blessed in Jesus, by the grace of God, that we ought to need no stimulus to good works. The forgiveness of our sins, the having been made for ever the children of God, the having before us the Father's house as our home, these blessings ought to be sufficient motives to constrain us in love and gratitude to serve God abundantly all the days of our life, and cheerfully also to give up, as He may call for it, that with which He has entrusted us of the things of this world. But whilst this is the case, the Lord nevertheless holds out to us in His Holy Word motives why we should serve Him, deny ourselves, use our property for Him, etc.; and the last mentioned passage is one of that kind. The verse is true, both with reference to the life that is now and that which is to come. If we have been sparingly using our property for Him, there will have been little treasure laid up in heaven, and therefore a small amount of capital will be found in the world to come, so far as regards reaping. Again, we shall reap bountifully if we seek to be rich towards God, by abundantly using our means for Him, whether in ministering to the necessities of the poor saints, or using otherwise our pecuniary means for His work.

Dear brethren, these are realities! Very shortly, will come the reaping time, and then will be the question, whether we shall reap *sparingly* or *bountifully*. But while this passage refers to the life hereafter, it also refers to the life that now is. Just as now the love of Christ constrains us to communicate of that with which the Lord entrusts us, so will be the present reaping, both with regard to spiritual and temporal things. Should there be found therefore in a brother the want of entering into his position as being merely a steward for the Lord in his calling, and should he give no heed to the admonitions of the Holy Ghost to communicate to those who are in need, or to help the work of God; then, can such a brother be surprised that he meets with great difficulties in his calling, and that he cannot get on? This is according to the Lord's Word. He is *sowing sparingly*, and he therefore *reaps sparingly*. But should *the love of Christ* constrain a brother, out of the earnings of his calling to sow bountifully, he will even in this life reap bountifully, both with regard to blessings in his soul and with regard to temporal things.

Consider in this connection the following passage, which, though taken from the Book of Proverbs, is not of a Jewish character, but true concerning believers under the present dispensation also: "*There is that scattereth, and yet increaseth; and there is that withholdeth more than is meet, but it tendeth to poverty. The liberal soul shall be made fat: and he that watereth shall be watered also himself*" (Proverbs 11:24-25).

(2) In connection with 1 Corinthians 16:2, I would also direct my brethren in the Lord to the promise made in Luke 6:38, "*Give and it shall be given unto you: good measure, pressed down, and shaken together, and running over, shall men give into your bosom. For with the same measure that ye mete withal it shall be measured to you again.*" This refers evidently to the present dispensation, and evidently in its primary meaning to temporal things. Now let anyone, *constrained by the love of Christ*, act according to this passage; let him on the first day of the week communicate as the Lord has prospered him, and he will see that the Lord will act according to what is contained in this verse. If pride constrain us to give, if self-righteousness make us liberal, if natural feeling induce us to communicate, or if we give whilst we are in a state of insolvency, not possessing more perhaps than ten shillings in the pound were our creditors to come upon us; then we cannot expect to have this verse fulfilled in our experience; nor should we give at any time for the sake of receiving again from others, according to this verse; but if indeed *the love of Christ constrain us* to communicate according to the ability which the Lord gives us, then we shall have this verse fulfilled in our experience, though this was not the motive that induced us to give. Somehow or other the Lord will abundantly repay us through the instrumentality of our fellow men, what we are doing for His poor saints, or in any way for His work; and we shall find that in the end we are not losers, even with reference to temporal things, whilst we communicate liberally of the things of this life.

Here it might be remarked: But if it be so, that even in this life, and with regard to temporal things it is true, that "*To him that gives shall be given, good measure, pressed down, and shaken together, and running over,*" and that "*He which soweth bountifully shall reap also bountifully,*" then in the end the most liberal persons would be exceedingly rich.

Concerning this we have to keep in mind, that the moment persons were to begin to give for the sake of receiving more back again from the Lord through the instrumentality of their fellow men, than they have given; or the moment persons wished to alter their way, and no more go on sowing bountifully, but sparingly, in order to increase their possessions, whilst God is allowing them to reap bountifully, the river of God's bounty towards them would no longer continue to flow. God had supplied them abundantly with means, because He saw them act as *stewards* for Him. He had entrusted them with a little which they used for Him, and He therefore entrusted them with more; and if they had continued to use the much also for Him, He would have still more abundantly used them as instruments to scatter abroad His bounties. The child of God must be willing to be a channel through which God's bounties flow, both with regard to temporal and spiritual things. This channel is narrow and shallow at first, it may be; yet there is room for some of the waters of God's bounty to pass through. And if we cheerfully yield ourselves as channels, for this purpose, then the channel becomes wider and deeper, and the waters of the bounty of God can pass through more abundantly. Dropping figurative language it is thus: At first we may be instrumental in communicating £5 or £10 or £20 or £50 or £100 or £200 per year, but afterwards double as much; and if we are still more faithful in our stewardship, after a year or two four times as much, afterwards perhaps eight times as much, at last perhaps twenty times or fifty times as much. We cannot limit the extent to which God may use us as instruments in communicating blessing, both temporal and spiritual, if we are willing to yield ourselves as instruments to the living God, and are *content to be only instruments, and to give Him all the glory.* But with regard to temporal things it will be thus, that if indeed we walk according to the mind of God in these things, whilst more and more we become instruments of blessing to others, we shall not seek to enrich ourselves, but be content when the last day of another year finds us still in the body, to possess no more than on the last day of the previous year, or even considerably less, whilst we have been, however, in the course of the year the instruments of communicating largely to others, through the means with which the Lord had entrusted us.

As to my own soul, by the grace of God it would be a burden to me to find, that I was increasing in earthly possession; for it would be a plain proof to me that I had not been acting as a *steward* for God, and had not been yielding myself as a channel for the waters of God's bounty to pass through. I also cannot but bear my testimony here, that in whatever feeble measure God has enabled me to act according to these truths for the last sixty-four years and a half, I have found it to be profitable, most profitable to my own soul, and, as to temporal things, I never was a loser in doing so, but I have most abundantly found the truth of 1 Corinthians 9:6, and Luke 6:38, and Proverbs 11:24-25, verified in my own experience. I only have to regret that I have acted so little according to what I have now been stating, but my godly purpose is, by the help of God, to spend the remainder of my days in practicing these truths more than ever; and I am sure, that, when I am brought to the close of my earthly pilgrimage, either by death, or by the appearing of our Lord Jesus, I shall not have the least regret in having done so, and I know that should I leave my dear child behind, the Lord will abundantly provide for her, and prove that there has been a better provision made for her than her father could have made, if he had sought to insure his life or lay up money for her....

On Partnership with God

> *"And truly our fellowship is with the Father, and with His Son Jesus Christ" (1 John 1:3).*

Observe: (1) The words "fellowship", "communion", "co-participation", and "partnership", mean the same. (2) The believer in the Lord Jesus does not only obtain forgiveness of all his sins (as he does through the shedding of the blood of Jesus, by faith in His name); does not only become a righteous one before God (through the righteousness of the Lord Jesus, by faith in His name); is not only begotten again, born of God, and partaker of the divine nature, and therefore a child of God and an heir of God; but he is also in fellowship or partnership with God. Now, so far as regards God, and our standing in the Lord Jesus, we have this blessing once for all; nor does it allow of either an increase or a decrease. Just as God's love to us believers, His children, is unalterably the same (whatever may be the manifestations of that love), and as His peace with us is the same (however much our peace may be disturbed), so it is also with regard to our being in fellowship or partnership with Him: it remains unalterably the same, so far as God is concerned. But then (3) there is an *experimental* fellowship, or partnership, with the Father and with His Son, which consists in this, that all which we possess in God, as being the partners with God, is brought down into our daily life, is enjoyed, experienced, and used. This *experimental* fellowship, or partnership, allows of an increase or a decrease, in the measure in which faith is in exercise, and in which we are entering into what we have received in the Lord Jesus. The measure in which we enjoy this *experimental* fellowship with the Father and with the Son is without limit; for without limit we may make use of our partnership with the Father and with the Son, and draw by prayer and faith out of the inexhaustible fullness which there is in God.

Let us take a few instances in order to see the practical working of this *experimental* partnership with the Father and with the Son. Suppose there are two believing parents who were not brought to the knowledge of the truth until some years after the Lord had given them several children. Their children were brought up in sinful, evil ways, whilst the parents did not know the Lord. Now the parents reap as they sowed. They suffer from having set an evil example before their children; for their children are unruly and behave most improperly. What is now to be done? Need such parents despair? No. The first thing they have to do is, to make confession of their sins to God, with regard to neglecting their children whilst they were themselves living in sin, and then to remember that they are in partnership with God, and therefore to be of good courage though they are in themselves still utterly insufficient for the task of managing their children. They have in themselves neither the wisdom, nor the patience, nor the long-suffering, nor the gentleness, nor the meekness, nor the love, nor the decision and firmness, nor anything else that may be needful in dealing with their children aright. But their Heavenly Father has all this. The Lord Jesus possesses all this. And they are in partnership with the Father, and with the Son, and therefore they can obtain by prayer and faith all they need out of the fullness of God. I say by *prayer* and *faith*, for we have to make known our need to God in prayer, ask His help, and then we have to believe that He will give us what we need. Prayer alone is not enough. We may pray never so much, yet if we do not believe that God will give us what we need, we have no reason to expect that we shall receive what we have asked for. So then these parents would need to ask God to give them the needful wisdom, patience, long-suffering, gentleness, meekness, love, decision, firmness, and whatever else they may judge they need. They may in humble boldness remind their Heavenly Father that His Word assures them that they are in partnership with Him, and, as they themselves are lacking in these particulars, ask Him to supply their need; and then they have to *believe* that God will do it, and they will receive according to their need.

Another instance: Suppose I am so situated in my business that day by day such difficulties arise, that I continually find that I take wrong steps, by reason of these great difficulties. How may the case be altered for the better? In myself I see no remedy for the difficulties. In looking at myself I can expect nothing but to make still further mistakes, and, therefore, trial upon trial seems to be before me. And yet I need not despair. The living God is my partner: I have not sufficient wisdom to meet these difficulties so as to be able to know what steps to take, but He is able to direct me. What I have, therefore, to do is this: in simplicity to spread my case before my Heavenly Father and my Lord Jesus. The Father and the Son are my partners. I have to tell out my heart to God, and to ask Him, that, as He is my partner, and I have no wisdom in myself to meet all the many difficulties which continually occur in my business, He would be pleased to guide and direct me, and to supply me with the needful wisdom; and then I have to *believe* that God will do so, and go with good courage to my business, and *expect* help from Him in the next difficulty that may come before me. *I have to look out for guidance,*

I have to expect counsel from the Lord; and, as assuredly as I do so, I shall have it; I shall find that I am not nominally, but really in partnership with the Father and with the Son.

Another instance: There are two believing parents with seven small children. The father works in a manufactory, but cannot earn more than ten shillings per week. The mother cannot earn anything. These ten shillings are too little for the supply of nourishing and wholesome food for seven growing children and their parents, and for providing them with the other necessaries of life. What is to be done in such a case? Surely not to find fault with the manufacturer, who may not be able to afford more wages, and much less to murmur against God; but the parents have in simplicity to tell God, their partner, that the wages of ten shillings a week are not sufficient in England to provide nine persons with all they need, that their health may not be injured. They have to remind God that He is not a hard master, not an unkind being, but a most loving Father, who has abundantly proved the love of His heart in the gift of His only begotten Son. And they have in childlike simplicity to ask Him, that either He would order it so, that the manufacturer may be able to allow more wages, or that the Lord would find them another place, where the father would be able to earn more; or that He would be pleased somehow or other, as it may seem good to Him, to supply them with more means. They have to ask the Lord, in childlike simplicity, again and again for it, if He does not answer their request at once; and they have *to believe* that God, their Father and partner, will give them the desire of their hearts. They have *to expect* an answer to their prayers; day by day they have *to look out* for it, and to repeat their request till God grants it. As assuredly as they *believe* that God will grant them their request, so assuredly it shall be granted.

Again, suppose I desire more power over my besetting sins; suppose I desire more power against certain temptations; suppose I desire more wisdom, or grace, or anything else that I may need in my service among the saints, or in my service towards the unconverted; what have I to do, but to make use of my being in fellowship with the Father and with the Son? Just as, for instance, an old faithful clerk, who is this day taken into partnership by an immensely rich firm, though himself altogether without property, would not be discouraged by reason of a large payment having to be made by the firm within three days, though he himself has no money at all of his own, but would comfort himself with the immense riches possessed by those who so generously have just taken him into partnership; so should we, the children of God and servants of Jesus Christ, comfort ourselves by being in fellowship, or partnership, with the Father, and with the Son, though we have no power of our own against our besetting sins; though we cannot withstand temptations which are before us, in our own strength; and though we have neither sufficient grace nor wisdom for our service among the saints, or towards the unconverted. All we have to do is, to draw upon our partner, the living God. By prayer and faith we may obtain all needful temporal and spiritual help and blessings. In all simplicity we have to tell out our heart before God, and then we have to believe that He will give to us according to our need. But *if we do not believe* that God will help us, could we be at peace? The clerk, taken into the firm as partner, *believes* that the firm will meet the payment though so large, and though in three days it is to be made, and it is this that keeps his heart quiet, though altogether poor himself. We have to believe that our infinitely rich partner, the living God, will help us in our need, and we shall not only be in peace, but we shall actually find that the help we need will be granted to us.

Let not the consciousness of your entire unworthiness keep you, dear reader, from believing what God has said concerning you. If you are indeed a believer in the Lord Jesus, then this precious privilege, being in partnership with the Father and the Son, is yours, though you and I are entirely unworthy of it. If the consciousness of our unworthiness were to keep us from believing what God has said concerning those who depend upon and trust in the Lord Jesus for salvation, then we should find that there is not one single blessing with which we have been blessed in the Lord Jesus from which, on account of our unworthiness, we could derive any settled comfort or peace.

On the Study of Scripture

–The Benefits of Meditation (1841)

While I was staying at Nailsworth, it pleased the Lord to teach me a truth, irrespective of human instrumentality, as far as I know, the benefit of which I have not lost, though now, while preparing the eighth edition for the press, more than forty years have since passed away. The point is this: I saw more clearly than ever, that the first great and primary business to which I ought to attend every day was, to have my soul happy in the Lord. The first thing to be concerned about was not, how much I might serve the Lord, how I might glorify the Lord; but how I might get my soul into a happy state, and how my inner man might be nourished. For I might seek to set the truth before the unconverted, I might seek to benefit believers, I might seek to relieve the distressed, I might in other ways seek to behave myself as it becomes a child of God in this world; and yet, not being happy in the Lord, and not being nourished and strengthened in my inner man day by day, all this might not be attended to in a right spirit. Before this time my practice had been, at least for ten years previously, as an habitual thing, to give myself to prayer, after having dressed in the morning.

Now I saw, that the most important thing I had to do was to give myself to the reading of the Word of God and to meditate on it, that thus my heart might be comforted, encouraged, warned, reproved, instructed; and that thus, whilst meditating, my heart might be brought into experimental communion with the Lord. I began, therefore, to meditate on the New Testament, from the beginning, early in the morning. The first thing I did, after having asked in a few words the Lord's blessing upon His precious Word, was to begin to meditate on the Word of God, searching, as it were, into every verse, to get blessing out of it; not for the sake of the public ministry of the Word; not for the sake of preaching on what I had meditated upon; but for the sake of obtaining food for my own soul. The result I have found to be almost invariably this, that after a very few minutes my soul has been led to confession, or to thanksgiving, or to intercession, or to supplication; so that though I did not, as it were, give myself to *prayer*, but to *meditation*, yet it turned almost immediately more or less into prayer. When thus I have been for awhile making confession, or intercession, or supplication, or have given thanks, I go on to the next words or verse, turning all, as I go on, into prayer for myself or others, as the Word may lead to it; but still continually keeping before me, that food for my own soul is the object of my meditation. The result of this is, that there is always a good deal of confession, thanksgiving, supplication, or intercession mingled with my meditation, and that my inner man almost invariably is even sensibly nourished and strengthened and that by breakfast time, with rare exceptions, I am in a peaceful if not happy state of heart. Thus also the Lord is pleased to communicate unto me that which, very soon after, I have found to become food for other believers, though it was not for the sake of the public ministry of the Word that I gave myself to meditation, but for the profit of my own inner man.

The difference then between my former practice and my present one is this: Formerly, when I rose, I began to pray as soon as possible, and generally spent all my time till breakfast in prayer, or almost all the time. At all events, I almost invariably began with prayer, except when I felt my soul to be more than usually barren, in which case I read the Word of God for food, or for refreshment, or for a revival and renewal of my inner man, before I gave myself to prayer. But what was the result? I often spent a quarter of an hour, or half an hour, or even an hour on my knees, before being conscious to myself of having derived comfort, encouragement, humbling of soul, etc.; and often, after having suffered much from wandering of mind for the first ten minutes, or a quarter of an hour, or even half an hour, I only then began *really to pray*. I scarcely ever suffer now in this way. For my heart being flourished by the truth, being brought into *experimental* fellowship with God, I speak to my Father, and to my Friend (vile though I am, and unworthy of it!) about the things that He has brought before me in His precious Word.

It often now astonishes me that I did not sooner see this. In no book did I ever read about it. No public ministry ever brought the matter before me. No private intercourse with a brother stirred me up to this matter. And yet now, since God has taught me this point, it is as plain to me as anything, that the first thing the child of God has to do morning by morning is to *obtain food for his inner man.* As the outward man is not fit for work for any length of time, except we take food, and as this is one of the first things we do in the morning, so it should be with the inner man. We should take food for that, as everyone must allow. Now what is the food for the inner man? Not *prayer,* but *the Word of God;* and here again not the simple reading of the Word of God, so that it only passes through our minds, just as water runs through a pipe, but considering what we read, pondering over it, and applying it to our hearts.

When we pray we speak to God. Now, prayer, in order to be continued for any length of time in any other than a formal manner, requires, generally speaking, a measure of strength or godly desire, and the season, therefore, when this exercise of the soul can be most effectually performed, is, after the inner man has been nourished by meditation on the Word of God, where we find our Father speaking to us, to encourage us, to comfort us, to instruct us, to humble us, to reprove us. We may therefore profitably meditate, with God's blessing, though we are ever so weak spiritually; nay, the weaker we are, the more we need meditation for the strengthening of our inner man. There is thus far less to be feared from wandering of mind, than if we give ourselves to prayer, without having had previously time for meditation.

I dwell so particularly on this point because of the immense spiritual profit and refreshment I am conscious of having derived from it myself, and I affectionately and solemnly beseech all my fellow believers to ponder this matter. By the blessing of God I ascribe to this mode the help and strength which I have had from God to pass in peace through deeper trials in various ways than I had ever had before; and after having now above forty years tried this way, I can most fully, in the fear of God, commend it. How different when the soul is refreshed and made happy early in the morning, from what it is when, without spiritual preparation, the service; the trials, and the temptations of the day come upon one!

–Preparation for Preaching (1830)

That which I now considered the best mode of preparation for the public ministry of the Word, from deep conviction, and from the experience of God's blessing upon it, is as follows: I ask the Lord that He would graciously be pleased to teach me on what subject I shall speak, or what portion of His Word I shall expound. Sometimes it happens that a subject, or a passage, has been in my mind; in that case I ask Him whether I should speak on it. If after prayer I feel persuaded that I should, I fix upon it, yet so that I would desire to leave myself open to the Lord to change it, if He please. Frequently, however, it occurs that I have no text or subject in my mind before I give myself to prayer. In this case I wait some time for an answer, trying to listen to the voice of the Spirit to direct me. If then a passage or subject is brought to my mind, I again ask Him, and that sometimes repeatedly, whether it be His will I should speak on it. Frequently it happens that I not only have no text or subject, but also do not obtain one after once or twice, or more times, praying about it. What I do is to go on with my regular reading of the Scriptures, praying whilst I read, for a text. I have even had to go to the place of meeting without a text, and obtained it perhaps only a few minutes before I was going to speak; but I have never lacked the Lord's assistance at the time of preaching, provided I had earnestly sought it in private.

Now when the text has been obtained, whether it be one or two or more verses, or a whole chapter, I ask the Lord that He would graciously be pleased to teach me by His Holy Spirit, whilst meditating over it. Within the last sixty-three years I have found it the most profitable plan to meditate with my pen in my hand, writing down the outlines, as the Word is opened to me. This I do for the sake of clearness, as being a help to see how far I understand the passage. I very seldom use any other help besides the little I understand of the original of the Scriptures, and some good translations in other languages. My chief help is prayer. I have *never* in my life begun to study one single part of divine truth without gaining some light about it, when I have been able really to give myself to prayer and meditation over it. This I most firmly believe, that no one ought to expect to see much good resulting from his labours if he is not much given to prayer and meditation.

That which I have found most beneficial in the public ministry of the Word, is *expounding* the Scriptures. This may be done in a twofold way, either by entering minutely into the bearing of every point occurring in the portion, or by giving the general outlines, and thus leading the hearers to see the meaning and connection of the whole. The benefits which I have seen resulting from *expounding* are these: (1) The hearers are thus, with God's blessing, led to the Scriptures. This induces them to bring their Bibles, and I have observed that those who did not bring them, have afterwards been induced to do so; so that in a short time few were in the habit of coming without them. This is no small matter; for everything which in our day will lead believers to value the Scriptures is of importance. (2) The *expounding* of the Scriptures is in general more beneficial to the hearers than if, on a single verse, or half a verse, or two or three words of a verse, some remarks are made, so that the portion of Scripture is scarcely anything but a motto for the subject. (3) The *expounding* of the Scriptures leaves to the hearers a connecting link, so that the reading over again the portion of the Word which had been expounded, brings to their remembrance what has been said; and thus, with God's blessing, leaves a more lasting impression on their minds. Expounding the Word of God brings little honour to the preacher from the *unenlightened* or *careless* hearer, but it tends much to the benefit of the hearers in general.

Simplicity of expression, whilst the truth is set forth, is of the utmost importance. It should be the aim of the teacher so to speak, that children, servants, and people who cannot read may be able to understand him, so far as the natural mind can comprehend the things of God. It should also be considered, that if the preacher strive to speak according to the rules of this world, he may please many, particularly those who have a literary taste, but in the same proportion he is less likely to become an instrument in the hands of God for the conversion of sinners or for the building up of the saints. For neither eloquence nor depth of thought makes the truly great preacher, but such a life of prayer, and meditation, and spirituality, as may render him *"a vessel meet for the Master's use,"* and fit to be employed both in the conversion of sinners and in the edification of the saints.

On Discerning the Will of God

> *Reprinted from* George Müller - Man of Faith and Miracles, *by Basil Miller, pp.50-51.*

Many asked Mr. Müller how he sought to know the will of God, in that nothing was undertaken, not even the smallest expenditure, without feeling certain he was in God's will. In the following words he gave his answer:

(1) I seek at the beginning to get my heart into such a state that it has not will of its own in regard to a given matter. Nine-tenths of the difficulties are overcome when our hearts are ready to do the Lord's will, whatever it may be. When one is truly in this state, it is usually but a little way to the knowledge of what His will is.

(2) Having done this, I do not leave the result to feeling or simple impressions. If so, I make myself liable to great delusions.

(3) I seek the will of the Spirit of God through or in connection with the Word of God. The Spirit and the Word must be combined. If I look to the Spirit alone without the Word, I lay myself open to great delusions also.

(4) Next I take into account providential circumstances. These plainly indicate God's will in connection with His Word and Spirit.

(5) I ask God in prayer to reveal His will to me aright.

(6) Thus through prayer to God, the study of the Word and reflection, I come to a deliberate judgment according to the best of my ability and knowledge, and if my mind is thus at peace, and continues so after two or three more petitions, I proceed accordingly. In trivial matters and in transactions involving most important issues, I have found this method always effective.

And did this plan work? one asks. Let Mr. Müller's testimony answer.

"I never remember," he wrote three years before his death, "in all my Christian course, a period now of sixty-nine years and four months, that I ever SINCERELY AND PATIENTLY sought to know the will of God by the teaching of the Holy Ghost, through the instrumentality of the Word of God, but I have been always directed rightly. But if honesty of heart and uprightness before God were lacking, or if I did not patiently wait upon God for instruction, or if I preferred the counsel of my fellow men to the declarations of the Word of the living God, I made great mistakes."

– III –

MÜLLER'S ENCOURAGEMENT TO THOSE WITH UNCONVERTED FAMILY AND FRIENDS

Reprinted from The Autobiography of George Müller, *Whitaker House, 1984, pp.135-138.*

For the encouragement of believers who are tried by having unconverted relatives and friends, I will relate the following circumstance which I know is true. Baron von Kamp, who lived in Prussia, had been a disciple of the Lord Jesus for many years. In the year 1806, great financial distress came upon many thousands of weavers in the area. They had no employment because the whole continent was in an unsettled state from the war . The baron believed that it was the will of the Lord to use his wealth to furnish these poor weavers with work, in order to save them from complete ruin. There was not only no prospect of personal gain, but rather the certain prospect of immense loss. Nevertheless, he found employment for about six thousand weavers.

But the baron was not content with this. He also wanted to minister to the souls of these weavers. He set believers as overseers over his immense weaving concern. The weavers were instructed in spiritual things, and he personally shared the truth of the gospel with them. The work went on for a good while until at last, on account of the loss of most of his property, he was obliged to think about giving it up. But by this time, his precious act of mercy had proven its worth to the government. It was taken up by them and carried on until the times changed. Baron von Kamp was appointed director of the whole concern as long as it existed.

This dear man of God was not content with this. He traveled through many countries to visit the prisons for the sake of improving the physical and spiritual condition of the prisoners. He also assisted poor students at the university of Berlin, especially those who studied theology , in order to win them for the Lord. One day a talented young man heard of the aged baron's kindness to students. He wrote to the baron, requesting his assistance because his own father could not afford to support him any longer. A short time afterward, young Thomas received a kind reply from the baron, inviting him to come to Berlin. But before this letter arrived, the young student had heard that Baron von Kamp was a "pietist" or "mystic," as true believers were contemptuously called in Germany. Young Thomas was deeply involved in philosophy, reasoning about everything, questioning the truth of revelation, questioning even the existence of God. He disliked the prospect of going to the old baron for help. Still, he thought he could try, and if he did not like it, he was not obligated to remain in connection with him. Thomas arrived in Berlin on a day when the baron was out of town on business. He began to speak about his philosophies to the steward of the baron. The steward, however, was a believer, and he turned the conversation to spiritual things. At last the baron arrived. He received Thomas in the most affectionate and familiar manner. The baron offered him a room in his house and a place at his table while Thomas studied in Berlin. Thomas accepted the offer. The baron now sought in every way to treat the young student in the most kind and affectionate way, to serve him as much as possible, and to show him the power of the gospel in his own life. He did all this without arguing with him or even speaking to him directly about his soul. Thomas obviously had a skeptical mind, and the baron avoided getting into any argument with him. The student often said to himself, "I wish I could get into an argument with this old fool. I would show him how irrational his beliefs are." But the baron avoided it. When the baron heard the young student come home in the evening, he would go to meet him and serve him in any way he could, even helping him to take off his boots. Thus this lowly, aged disciple went on for some time. While Thomas still sought an opportunity for arguing with him, he wondered how the baron could continue to serve him. One evening when Thomas returned to the baron's house, the baron was making himself his servant as usual. The student could restrain himself no longer and burst out, "Baron, how can you do all this? You see I do not care about you. How are you able to continue to be so kind to me and serve me like this?" The baron replied, "My dear young friend, I have learned it from the Lord Jesus. I wish you would read through the gospel of John. Good night." The student now for the first time in his life sat down and read the Word of God with an open heart and a willingness to learn. Up to that time, he had never read the Holy Scriptures unless he wanted to find out arguments against them. God blessed him. From that time he became a follower of the Lord Jesus and has continued in the faith ever since.

– IV –

AN ADDRESS TO YOUNG CONVERTS

As one who for fifty years has known the Lord, and has laboured in word and doctrine, I ought to be able, in some little measure, to lend a helping hand to these younger believers. And if God will only condescend to use the acknowledgment of my own failures to which I refer, and of my experience, as a help to others in walking on the road to heaven, I trust that your coming here will not be in vain. This was the very purpose of my leaving home—that I might help these dear young brethren.

The Manner of Reading the Word

One of the most deeply important points is that of attending to the careful, prayerful reading of the Word of God, and meditation thereon. I would therefore ask your particular attention to one verse in the Epistle of Peter (1 Peter 2:2), where we are especially exhorted by the Holy Ghost through the apostle, regarding this subject. For the sake of the connection, let us read the first verse, "*Wherefore laying aside all malice, and all guile and hypocrisies, and envies, and all evil-speakings, as new-born babes, desire the sincere milk of the Word, that ye may grow thereby; if so be ye have tasted that the Lord is gracious.*"

The particular point to which I refer is contained in the second verse, "*as new-born babes, desire the sincere milk of the Word.*" As growth in the natural life is attained by proper food, so in the spiritual life, if we desire to grow, this growth is only to be attained through the instrumentality of the Word of God. It is not stated here, as some might be very willing to say, that "the reading of the Word may be of importance under some circumstances." Nor is it stated that you may gain profit by reading the statement which is [being] made here; it is of the 'Word,' and of the Word alone, that the apostle speaks, and nothing else.

Cleave to the Word of God

You say that the reading of this tract or of that book often does you good. I do not question it. Nevertheless, the instrumentality which God has been specially pleased to appoint and to use is that of *the Word itself*; and just in the measure in which the disciples of the Lord Jesus Christ attend to this, they will become strong in the Lord; and in so far as it is neglected, so far will they be weak. There is such a thing as babes being neglected, and what is the consequence? They never become healthy men or women, because of that early neglect.

Perhaps—and it is one of the most hurtful forms of this neglect—they obtain improper food, and therefore do not attain the full vigor of maturity. So with regard to the divine life. It is a most deeply important point, that we obtain right spiritual food at the very beginning of that life. What is that food? It is "*the sincere milk of the Word*" that is the proper nourishment for the strengthening of the new life. Listen, then, my dear brethren and sisters, to some advice with regard to the Word.

Consecutive Reading

First of all, it is of the utmost moment that we read regularly through the Scripture. We ought not to turn over the Bible, and pick out chapters as we please here and there, but we should read it carefully and regularly through. I speak advisedly, and as one who has known the blessedness of thus reading the Word for the last forty-six years. I say *forty-six* years, because for the first four years of my Christian life I did not carefully read the Word of God. I used to read a tract, or an interesting book, but I knew nothing of the power of the Word. I read very little of it, and the result was, that, although a preacher then, yet I made no progress in the divine life. And why? Just for this reason—I neglected the Word of God.

But it pleased God, through the instrumentality of a beloved Christian brother, to rouse in me an earnestness about the Word, and ever since then I have been a lover of it.

Let me, then, press upon you my first point, that of attending regularly to reading through the Scriptures. I do not suppose that you *all* need the exhortation. Many, I believe, have already done so, but I speak for the benefit of those who have not. To those I say, 'My dear friends, begin at once.' Begin with the Old Testament, and when you have read a chapter or two, and are about to leave off, put a mark that you may know where you have left off. I speak in all simplicity for the benefit of those who may be young in the divine life. The next time you read, begin the New Testament, and again put a mark where you leave off. And thus go on, always reading alternately the Old and the New Testaments. Thus, by little and little, you will read through the whole Bible; and when you have finished, begin again at the beginning.

The Connection of Scripture

Why is this so deeply important? Simply that we may see *the connection* between one book and another of the Bible, and between one chapter and another. If we do not read in this consecutive way, we lose a great part of what God has given to instruct us. Moreover, if we are children of God, we should be well acquainted with the whole revealed will of God—the whole of the Word. *"All Scripture is given by inspiration, and is profitable."* And much may be gained by thus carefully reading through the whole of the revealed will of God. Suppose a rich relative were to die, and leave us, perhaps, some land, or houses, or money, should we be content with reading only the clauses that affected us particularly? No, we would be careful to read the whole will right through. How much more, then, with regard to the revealed will of God ought we to be careful to read it through, and not merely one and another of the chapters or books.

Another Benefit of this Consecutive Reading

And this careful reading of the Word of God has this advantage, that it keeps us from making *a system of doctrine of our own*, and from having our own particular favorite views, which is very pernicious. We often are apt to lay too much stress on certain views of the truth which affect us particularly. The will of the Lord is that we should know *His whole revealed mind*. Again, variety in the things of God is of great moment. And God has been pleased to give us this variety in the highest degree; and the child of God, who follows out this plan, will be able to take an interest in every part of the Word.

Suppose one says, "Let us read in Leviticus." Very well, my brother. Suppose another says, "Let us read in the prophecy of Isaiah." Very well, my brother. And another will say, "Let us read in the gospel according to Matthew." Very well, my brother; I can enjoy them all; and whether it be in the Old Testament, or in the New Testament, whether in the Prophets, the Gospels, the Acts, or the Epistles, I should welcome it, and be delighted to welcome the reading and study of any part of the divine Word.

Specially Beneficial to the Labourer for Christ

And this will be of particular advantage to us, in case we should become *labourers in Christ's vineyard*; because in expounding the Word, we shall be able to refer to every part of it. We shall equally enjoy the reading of the Word, whether of the Old or the New Testament, and shall never get tired of it. I have, as before stated, known the blessedness of this plan for forty-six years, and though I am now nearly seventy years of age, and though I have been converted for nearly fifty years, I can say, by the grace of God, that I more than ever love the Word of God, and have greater delight than ever in reading it. And though I have read the Word nearly a hundred times right through. I have never got tired of reading it, and this is more especially through reading it regularly, consecutively, day by day, and not merely reading a chapter here and there, as my own thoughts might have led me to do.

Reading the Word Prayerfully

Again, we should read the Scripture *prayerfully*, never supposing that we are clever enough or wise enough to understand God's Word by our own wisdom. In all our reading of the Scriptures let us seek carefully to have the help of the Holy Spirit; let us ask, for Jesus' sake, that He will enlighten us. He is willing to do it. I will tell you how it fared with me at the very first; it may be for your encouragement. It was in the year 1829, when I was living in Hackney. My attention had been called to the teaching of the Spirit by a dear brother of experience. "Well," I said, "I will try this plan ; and will give myself, after prayer, to the careful reading of the Word of God, and to meditation, and I will see how much the Spirit is willing to teach me in this way."

An Illustration of This

I went accordingly to my room, and locked my door, and putting the Bible on a chair, I went down on my knees at the chair. There I remained for several hours in prayer and meditation over the Word of God; and I can tell you that I learned more in those three hours which I spent in this way, than I had learned for many months previously. I thus obtained the teaching of the

Divine Spirit, and I cannot tell you the blessedness which it was to my own soul. I was praying in the Spirit, and putting my trust in the power of the Spirit, as I had never done before. You cannot, therefore, be surprised at my earnestness in pressing this upon you, when you have heard how precious to my heart it was, and how much it helped me.

Meditate on the Word

But again, it is not enough to have prayerful reading only, but we must also meditate on the Word. As in the instance I have just referred to, kneeling before the chair, I meditated on the Word. It was not simply reading it, not simply praying over it. It was all that, but, in addition it was pondering over what I had read. This is deeply important. If you merely read the Bible, and no more, it is just like water running in at one side and out at the other. In order to be really benefitted by it, we must meditate on it. We cannot all of us, of course, spend many hours, or even one or two hours each day in this manner. Our business demands our attention. Yet, however short the time you can afford, give it regularly to reading, prayer and meditation over the Word, and you will find it will well repay you.

Make the Meditation Personal

In connection with this, we should always read and meditate over the Word of God, with reference to ourselves and our own heart. This is deeply important, and I cannot press it too earnestly upon you. We are apt often to read the Word with reference to others. Parents read it in reference to their children, children for their parents; evangelists read it for their congregations, Sunday-school teachers for their classes. Oh! this is a poor way of reading the Word; if read in this way, it will not profit. I say it deliberately and advisedly, the sooner it is given up, the better for your own souls. Read the Word of God always *with reference to your own heart*, and when you have received the blessing in your own heart, you will be able to communicate it to others.

Whether you labour as evangelists, as pastors, or as visitors, superintendents of Sunday schools, or teachers, tract distributors or in whatever other capacity you may seek to labour for the Lord, be careful to let the reading of the Word be with distinct reference to your own heart. Ask yourselves, how does this suit *me*, either for instruction, for correction, for exhortation, or for rebuke? How does this affect me? If you thus read, and get the blessing in your own soul, how soon it will flow out to others!

Read in Faith

Another point. It is of the utmost moment in reading the Word of God, that the reading should be accompanied *with faith*. "*The word preached did not profit them; not being mixed with faith in them that heard it.*" As with the preaching, so with the reading; it must be mixed with faith. Not simply reading it as you would read a story, which you may receive or not; not simply as a statement, which you may credit or not; or as an exhortation, to which you may listen or not; but as the *revealed will of the Lord*: that is, receiving it *with faith*. Received thus, it will nourish us, and we shall reap benefit. Only in this way will it benefit us; and we shall gain from it health and strength in proportion as we receive it with real faith.

Be Doers of the Word

Lastly, if God does bless us in reading His Word, He expects that we should be *obedient* children, and that we should accept the Word as His will, and carry it into practice. If this be neglected, you will find that the reading of the Word, even if accompanied by prayer, meditation and faith, will do you little good. God does expect us to be obedient children, and will have us practice what He has taught us. The Lord Jesus Christ says: "*If ye know these things, happy are ye if ye do them.*" And in the measure in which we carry out what our Lord Jesus taught, so much in measure are we happy children. And in such measure only can we honestly look for help from our Father, even as we seek to carry out His will. If there is one single point I would wish to have spread all over this country, and over the whole world, it is just this, that we should seek, beloved Christian friends, not to be hearers of the Word only, but "*doers of the Word.*" I doubt not that many of you have sought to do this already, but I speak particularly to those younger brethren and sisters who have not yet learned the full force of this. Oh! seek to attend earnestly to this, it is of vast importance. Satan will seek with much earnestness to put aside the Word of God; but let us seek to carry it out and to act upon it. The Word must be received as a legacy from God, which has been communicated to us by the Holy Ghost.

The Fullness of the Revelation Given in the Word

And remember that, to the faithful reader of this blessed Word, it reveals all that we need to know about the Father, all that we need to know about the Lord Jesus Christ, all about the power of the Spirit, all about the world that lieth in the wicked one, all about the road to heaven, and the blessedness of the world to come. In this blessed book we have the whole Gospel, and all rules necessary for our Christian life and warfare. Let us see then that we study it with our whole heart and with prayer, meditation, faith and obedience.

Prayer

The next point on which I will speak for a few moments has been more or less referred to already, it is that of prayer. You might read the Word and seem to understand it very fully, yet if you are not in the habit of waiting continually upon God, you will make little progress in the divine life. We have not naturally in us any good thing, and cannot expect, save by the help of God, to please Him. Therefore, it is the will of the Lord that we should always own our dependence upon Him in prayer. The blessed Lord Jesus Christ gave us an example in this particular. He gave whole nights to prayer. We find Him on the lonely mountain engaged by night in prayer. And as in every way He is to be an example to us, so, in particular, on this point. He is an example to us. The old evil corrupt nature is still in us, though we are born again; therefore, we have to come in prayer to God for help. We have to cling to the power of the Mighty One. Concerning everything, we have to pray. Not simply when great troubles come, when the house is on fire, or a beloved wife is on the point of death, or dear children are laid down in sickness— not simply at such times, but also *in little things.*

From the very early morning, let us make *everything* a matter of prayer, and let it be so throughout the day, and throughout our whole life. A Christian lady said lately, that thirty-five years ago she heard me speak on this subject in Devonshire; and that then I referred to praying about little things. I had said, that suppose a parcel came to us, and it should prove difficult to untie the knot, and you cannot cut it; then you should ask God to help you, even to untie the knot. I myself had forgotten the words, but she has remembered them, and the remembrance of them, she said, had been a great help to her again and again. So I would say to you, my beloved friends, there is nothing too little to pray about. In the simplest things connected with our daily life and walk, we should give ourselves to prayer; and we shall have the living, loving Lord Jesus to help us. Even in the most trifling matters I give myself to prayer and often in the morning, even ere I leave my room I have two or three answers to prayer in this way.

Young believers, in the very outset of the divine life in your souls, learn, in childlike simplicity, to wait upon God for everything! Treat the Lord Jesus Christ as *your personal Friend*, able and willing to help you in everything. How blessed it is to be carried in His loving arms all the day long! I would say that the divine life of the believer is made up of a vast number of little circumstances and little things. Every day there comes before us a variety of little trials, and if we seek to put them aside in our own strength and wisdom, we shall quickly find that we are confounded. But if, on the contrary, we take everything to God, we shall be helped, and our way shall be made plain. Thus our life will be a happy life!

A Word to the Unconverted

I am here tonight addressing believers, those who have felt the burden of their sins, and have accepted Christ as their Savior, and who now through Him have peace with God and seek to glorify Him. But if there be any here who are still in their sins, in a state of alienation from God, let me say, if they die in this state, the terrible punishment of sin must fall upon them. Unless their sins are pardoned, and they are made fit for the Divine presence, they can never enter heaven. But, dear friends, Christ came to save the lost, and as sinners, you are lost, and you have no power of your own to save yourselves. The world talks of turning over a new leaf, but that will not satisfy Divine justice. Sin must be punished, or God's righteousness would be set aside. Jesus came into the world to bear that punishment. He has borne it in our room and stead. He has suffered for us. Now what God looks for from us is that we accept Jesus as our Savior, and put our trust in Him for the salvation of our souls. Whosoever looks really and entirely to Him shall assuredly be saved. Let his sins be ever so many, he shall have the forgiveness of them all. Nay, more, he will be accepted by God as His child. He will become an heir of God and a joint-heir with Christ. Oh, what a great and glorious salvation, so freely given! May it be as thankfully accepted! And may we who rejoice in Him, stand boldly out and confess Christ, and work for Him. May we not be half-hearted, but be valiant soldiers of Christ.

Let us be decided for Christ. Let us walk as in God's sight, in holy, peaceful, happy fellowship with Him, in the enjoyment of that nearness into which we are brought in Christ. Oh, the blessedness of this privilege of living near to God in this life! May we, then, seek His guidance in everything, so that we may be a blessing to others, and thus we shall be greatly blessed in our own souls.

– V –

A FEW HELPFUL EXCERPTS FROM THE JOURNAL OF GEORGE MÜLLER

Beginning Steps of Faith

The following are only a few journal entries from Mr. Müller's early years of learning to trust God for personal needs.

–Forgoes a Stated Salary (1830)

About this time I began to have conscientious objections against any longer receiving a stated salary.... A box was put up in the chapel, over which was written, that whoever had a desire to do something towards my support, might put his offering into the box.

At the same time it appeared to me right, that henceforth I should ask no man, not even my beloved brethren and sisters, to help me, as I had done a few times according to their own request, as my expenses, on account of traveling much in the Lord's service, were too great to be met by my usual income. For unconsciously I had thus again been led, in some measure, to trust in an arm of flesh; going to man instead of going to the Lord at once. *To come to this conclusion before God, required more grace than to give up my salary.* About the same time also my wife and I had grace given to us to take the Lord's commandment, "*Sell that ye have, and give alms*" (Luke 12:33), literally, and to carry it out. Our staff and support in this matter were Matthew 6:19-34 and John 14:13-14. We leaned on the arm of the Lord Jesus. *(It is now sixty-four years since we set out in this way, and we do not in the least regret the step we then took.* Our God also has, in His tender mercy, given us grace to abide in the same mind concerning the above points, both as regards principle and practice; and this has been the means of letting us see the tender love and care of our God over His children, even in the most minute things, in a way in which we never experimentally knew them before; and it has, in particular, made the Lord known to us more fully than we knew Him before, as *a prayer-hearing God.)*

–Financial Trials and Deliverances (1830)

November 18th, 1830. Our money was reduced to about eight shillings. When I was praying with my wife in the morning, the Lord brought to my mind the state of our purse, and I was led to ask Him for some money. About four hours after, we were with a sister at Bishopsteignton, and she said to me, "Do you want any money?" I said, "I told the brethren, dear sister, when I gave up my salary, that I would for the future tell the Lord only about my wants." She replied, "But He has told me to give you some money. About a fortnight ago I asked Him what I should do for Him, and He told me to give you some money; and last Saturday it came again powerfully to my mind, and has not left me since, and I felt it so forcibly last night that I could not help speaking of it to Brother P." My heart rejoiced, seeing the Lord's faithfulness, but I thought it better not to tell her about our circumstances, lest she should be influenced to give accordingly; and I also was assured that, if it were of the Lord, she could not but give. I therefore turned the conversation to other subjects, but when I left she gave me two guineas. We were full of joy on account of the goodness of the Lord. I would call upon the reader to admire the gentleness of the Lord, that He did not try our faith much at the commencement, but gave us first encouragement, and allowed us to see His willingness to help us, before He was pleased to try it more fully....

Between Christmas and the New Year, when our money was reduced to a few shillings, I asked the Lord for more; when a few hours after there was given to us a sovereign by a brother from Axminster. This brother had heard much against me, and was at last determined to hear for himself, and thus came to Teignmouth, a distance of forty miles; and, having heard about our manner of living, gave us this money.

With this closes the year 1830. Throughout it the Lord richly supplied all my temporal wants, though at the commencement of it I had no certain human prospect of one single shilling; so that, even as regards temporal things, I had not been in the smallest degree a loser in acting according to the dictates of my conscience, and as regards spiritual things, the Lord has indeed dealt bountifully with me, and led me on in many respects, and, moreover, had condescended to use me as an instrument in doing His work.

–Tempted to Unbelief (1831)

On January 6th, 7th, and 8th, 1831, I had repeatedly asked the Lord for money, but received none. On the evening of January 8th I left my room for a few minutes, and was then tempted to distrust the Lord, though He had been so gracious to us, in that He not only up to that day had supplied all our wants, but had given us also those answers to prayer, which have been in part just mentioned. I was so sinful, for about five minutes, as to think it would be of no use to trust in the Lord in this way. I also began to say to myself, that I had perhaps gone too far in living in this way. But thanks to the Lord! This trial lasted but a few minutes. He enabled me again to trust in Him, and Satan was immediately confounded; for when I returned to my room (out of which I had not been absent ten minutes), the Lord had sent deliverance, for a sister in the Lord, who resided at Exeter, had come to Teignmouth, and brought us £2 4s.

January 10th. Today, when we had again but a few shillings, £5 was given to us, which had been taken out of the box. I had, once for all, told the brethren, who had the care of these temporal things, to have the kindness to let me have the money every week; but as these beloved brethren either forgot to take it out weekly, or were ashamed to bring it in such small sums, it was generally taken out every three, four, or five weeks. As I had stated to them, however, from the commencement that I desired to look neither to man nor the box, but to the living God, I thought it not right on my part to remind them of my request to have the money weekly, lest it should hinder the testimony which I wished to give, of trusting in the living God alone.

It was on this account that on *January 28th*, when we had again but little money, though I had seen the brethren on January 24th open the box and take out the money, I would not ask the brother in whose hands it was, to let me have it; but I asked the Lord to incline his heart to bring it, and but a little time afterwards it was given to us, even £1 88. 6d.

On *March 7th* I was again *tempted* to disbelieve the faithfulness of the Lord, and though I was not miserable, still I was not so fully resting upon the Lord, that I could triumph with joy. It was *but one hour after*, when the Lord gave me another proof of His faithful love. There came from some sisters in the Lord, £5, with these words written on the paper:

"I was an hungered, and ye gave me meat; I was thirsty, and ye gave me drink. Lord, when saw we thee an hungered, and fed thee? or thirsty, and gave thee drink? The King shall answer and say unto them, Verily, verily I say unto you, inasmuch as ye have done it unto one of the least of these my brethren ye have done it unto me."

About *April 20th* I went to Chulmleigh. Here, and in the neighbourhood, I preached repeatedly, and from thence I went to Barnstaple. Whilst we were at Barnstaple there was found in my wife's bag a sovereign, put there anonymously. A sister also gave us £2.

On our return to Teignmouth, *May 2nd*, when we emptied our traveling bag, there fell out a paper with money. It contained two sovereigns and three pence, the latter put in, no doubt, to make a noise in emptying the bag. May the Lord bless and reward the giver! In a similar way we found 4s. put anonymously into one of our drawers, a few days after.

June 12th, Lord's day. On Thursday last I went with brother Craik to Torquay, to preach there. I had only about 3s. with me, and left my wife with about 6s. at home. The Lord provided beds for us through the hospitality of a brother. I asked the Lord repeatedly for money; but when I came home my wife had only about 3s. left, having received nothing. We waited still upon the Lord. Yesterday passed away and no money came. We had 9d. left. This morning we were still waiting upon the Lord, and looking for deliverance. We had only a little butter left for breakfast, sufficient for brother E. and a relative living with us, to whom we did not mention our circumstances, that they might not be made uncomfortable. After the morning meeting, Brother Y. most unexpectedly opened the box, and, in giving me quite as unexpectedly the money at such a time, he told me that *he and his wife could not sleep last night on account of thinking that we might want money.* The most striking point is, that after I had repeatedly asked the Lord, but received nothing, *I then prayed yesterday that the Lord would be pleased to impress it on brother Y. that we wanted money, so that he might open the box.* There was in it £1 8s. 10 1/2d. Our joy on account of this fresh deliverance was great, and we praised the Lord heartily.

July 20th. A shoulder of mutton and a loaf were sent to us anonymously. I understood some time afterwards, that Satan had raised the false report that we were starving, in consequence of which a believer sent these provisions. I would mention, by the way, that various reports have been circulated, on account of this our way of living. Sometimes it has been said that we had not enough to eat, and that surely such and such an infirmity of body we had brought on us, because we had not the necessaries of life. Now, the truth is, that, whilst we have been often brought low; yea, so low, that we have not had even as much as one single penny left; or so as to have the last loaf on the table, and not as much money as was needed to buy another loaf; yet never have we had to sit down to a meal, without our good Lord having provided *nourishing* food for us. I am bound to state this, and I do it *with pleasure*. My Master has been a kind Master to me, and if I had to choose this day again, as to the way of living, the Lord giving me grace, I would not choose differently. But even these very reports, false as they were, I doubt not the Lord has sometimes used as a means to put it into the hearts of His children, to remember our temporal necessities....

November 27th, Lord's day. Our money had been reduced to 2d.; our bread was hardly enough for this day. I had several times brought our need before the Lord. After dinner, when I returned thanks, I asked Him to give us our daily bread, meaning literally that He would send us bread for the evening. Whilst I was praying, there was a knock at the door of the room. After I had concluded, a poor sister came in, and brought us some of her dinner, and from another poor sister, 5s. In the afternoon she also brought us a large loaf. Thus the Lord not only literally gave us bread, but also money....

After we had, on *December 31st, 1831*, looked over the Lord's gracious dealings with us during the past year, in providing for all our temporal wants, we had about 10s. left. A little while after, the providence of God called for that, so that not a single farthing remained. Thus we closed the old year, in which the Lord had been so gracious in giving to us, without our asking anyone, altogether, £131 18s. 8d. There had been likewise many articles of provision and some articles of clothing given to us, worth at least £20. I am so particular in mentioning these things, to show that we are never losers by acting according to the mind of the Lord. For had I had my regular salary, humanly speaking, I should not have had nearly as much; but whether this would have been the case or not, this is plain, that I have not served a hard Master, and that is what I delight to show. For, to speak well of His name, that thus my beloved fellow-pilgrims, who may read this, may be encouraged to trust in Him, is the chief purpose of my writing.

Trusting God for Countless Others

The following are a few journal entries regarding God's establishment and care for the several orphan houses and thousands of orphans in Bristol. We have specifically chosen a time of crisis to demonstrate how God met the needs of His people on a daily basis.

–A Solemn Crisis. (1838)

September 10th. Monday morning. Neither Saturday nor yesterday had any money come in. It appeared to me now needful to take some steps on account of our need, *i.e.*, to go to the Orphan Houses, call the brethren and sisters together (who, except brother T—, had never been informed about the state of the funds), state the case to them, see how much money was needed for the present, tell them that amidst all this trial of faith I still believed that God would help, and to pray with them. Especially, also, I meant to go for the sake of telling them that no more articles must be purchased than we have the means to pay for, but to let there be nothing lacking in any way for the children as regards nourishing food and needful clothing; for I would rather at once send them away than that they should lack. I meant to go for the sake also of seeing whether there were still articles remaining which had been sent for the purpose of being sold, or whether there were any articles really needless, that we might turn them into money. I felt that the matter was now come to a solemn crisis.— About half-past nine sixpence came in, which had been put anonymously into the box at Gideon Chapel. This money seemed to me like an earnest, that God would have compassion and send more. About ten, after I had returned from brother Craik, to whom I had unbosomed my heart again, whilst once more in prayer for help, a sister called who gave two sovereigns to my wife for the Orphans, stating that she had felt herself stirred up to come, and that she had delayed coming already too long. A few minutes after, when I went into the room where she was, she gave me two sovereigns more, and all this without knowing the least about our need. Thus the Lord most mercifully has sent us a little help, to the great encouragement of my faith. A few minutes after I was called on for money from the Infants' Orphan House, to which I sent £2, and £1 0s. 6d. to the Boys' Orphan House, and £1 to the Girls' Orphan House. Today I saw a young brother who, as well as one of his sisters, had been brought to the knowledge of the Lord through my *Narrative*.

September 13th. This morning I found it was absolutely needful to tell the brethren and sisters about the state of the funds, and to give directions as to not going into debt, etc. We prayed together, and had a very happy meeting. They all seemed comfortable. There was 12s. 6d. taken out of the boxes in the three houses, 12s. one of the labourers gave, and £1 1s. had come in for needlework done by the children. One of the sisters, who is engaged in the work, sent a message after me, not to trouble myself about her salary, for she should not want any for a twelvemonth. What a blessing to have such fellow-labourers!

September 14th. I met again this morning with the brethren and sisters for prayer, as the Lord has not yet sent help. After prayer one of the labourers gave me all the money he had, 16s., saying that it would not be upright to pray, if he were not to give what he had. One of the sisters told me, that in six days she would give £6, which she had in the Savings' Bank for such a time of need. God be praised for such fellow-labourers! —Up to this day the matrons of the three houses had been in the habit of paying the bakers and the milkman weekly, *because they had preferred to receive the payments in this way*, and sometimes it had thus been also with the butcher and grocer. But, now, as the Lord deals out to us *by the day*, we considered it would be wrong to go on any longer in this way, as the week's payment might become due, and we have no money to meet it; and thus those with whom we deal might be inconvenienced by us, and we be found acting against the commandment of the Lord, "*Owe no man anything*" (Romans 13:8). From this day, and henceforward, whilst the Lord gives to us our supplies by the day, we purpose therefore to pay at once for every article as it is purchased, and never to buy anything except we can pay for it at once, however much it may seem to be needed, and however much those with whom we deal may wish to be paid only by the week. The little which was owed was paid off this day. When I came home I found a large parcel of new clothes, which, had been sent from Dublin for the Orphans, a proof that the Lord remembers us still. We met again in the evening for prayer. We were of good cheer, and still BELIEVE that the Lord will supply our need.

September 15th. Saturday. We met again this morning for prayer. God comforts our hearts. We are looking for help. I found that there were provisions enough for today and tomorrow, but there was no money in hand to take in bread as usual in order that the children might not have newly-baked bread. This afternoon one of the labourers, who had been absent for several days from Bristol, returned, and gave £1. This evening we met again for prayer, when I found that 10s. 6d. more had come in since the morning. With this £1 10s. 6d. we were able to buy, even this Saturday evening, the usual quantity of bread, and have some money left. God be praised, who gave us grace to come to the decision not to take any bread today, as usual, nor to buy anything for which we cannot pay at once.

September 17th. The trial still continues. It is now more and more trying, even to faith, as each day comes. Truly, the Lord has wise purposes in allowing us to call so long upon Him for help. But I am sure God will send help, if we can but wait. One of the labourers had had a little money come in, of which he gave 12s. 6d.; another labourer gave 11s. 8d., being all the money she had left: this, with 17s. 6d., which, partly, had come in, and, partly, was in hand, enabled us to pay what needed to be paid, and to purchase provisions, so that nothing yet, in any way has been lacking.

This evening I was rather tried respecting the long delay of larger sums coming; but being led to go to the Scriptures for comfort, my soul was greatly refreshed, and my faith again strengthened, by the 34th Psalm, so that I went very cheerfully to meet with my dear fellow-labourers for prayer. I read to them the Psalm, and sought to cheer their hearts through the precious promises contained in it.

–Come to Extremities

September 18th. Brother T. had 25s. in hand, and I had 3s. This £1 8s. enabled us to buy the meat and bread, which was needed; a little tea for one of the houses, and milk for all; no more than this is needed. Thus the Lord has provided not only for this day, but there is bread for two days in hand. Now, however, we are come to an extremity. The funds are exhausted. The labourers who had a little money have given as long as they had any left. Now observe how the Lord helped us! A lady from the neighbourhood of London who brought a parcel with money from her daughter, arrived four or five days since in Bristol, and took lodgings next door to the Boys' Orphan House. This afternoon she herself kindly brought me the money, amounting to £3 2s. 6d. We had been reduced so low as to be on the point of selling those things which could be spared; but this morning I had asked the Lord, if it might be, to prevent the necessity of our doing so. That the money had been so near the Orphan Houses for several days without being given, is a plain proof that it was from the beginning in the heart of God to help us; but, because He delights in the prayers of His children, He had allowed us to pray so long; also to try our faith, and to make the answer so much the sweeter. It is indeed a precious deliverance. I burst out into loud praises and thanks the first moment I was alone, after I had received the money. I met with my fellow-labourers again this evening for prayer and praise; their hearts were not a little cheered.

September 20th. Morning. The Lord has again kindly sent in a little. Last evening was given to me 1s. 6d., and this morning £1 3s. Evening. This evening the Lord sent still further supplies; £8 11s. 2½d. came in, as a further proof that the Lord is not unmindful of us. There was in the box of the Girls' Orphan House £1 1s., and in that of the Boys' Orphan House £1 7s. 2½d. One of the labourers, in accordance with her promise this day week, gave £6 3s. About eighteen months ago she saw it right no longer to have money for herself in the Savings' Bank, and she therefore, in her heart, gave the money which she had there to the Orphan Houses, intending to draw it in a time of need. Some time since (she told me this evening) she drew a part of it to buy several useful articles for the Orphan Houses; now the sum was reduced to £6. When she found out the present need, she went this day week to the Savings' Bank, and gave notice that she wished to draw her money today. Truly, as long as God shall be pleased to give me such fellow-labourers, His blessing will rest upon the work. This £8 11s. 2½d. was divided this evening to supply the three houses, and we thanked God, unitedly, for His help.

September 29th. Saturday evening. Prayer has been made for several days past respecting the rent, which is due this day. I have been looking out for it, though I knew not whence a shilling was to come. This morning brother T. called on me, and, as no money had come in, we prayed together, and continued in supplication from ten till a quarter to twelve. Twelve o'clock struck (the time when the rent ought to have been paid), but no money had been sent. For some days past I have repeatedly had a misgiving, whether the Lord might not disappoint us, in order that we might be led *to provide by the week, or the day, for the rent.* This is the second, and only the second, complete failure as to answers of prayer in the work, during the past four years and six months. The first was about the half-yearly rent of the Castle-Green school room, due July 1st, 1837, which had come in only in part by that time. I am now fully convinced that the rent ought to be put by daily or weekly, as God may prosper us, in order that the work, even as to this point, may be a testimony. May the Lord, then, help us to act accordingly; and may He now mercifully send in the means to pay the rent! Whilst in this matter our prayers have failed, either to humble us, or to show us how weak our faith is still, or to teach us (*which seems to me the most probable*) that we ought to provide the rent beforehand; the Lord has given us again fresh proofs, even this day, that He is mindful of us. There was not money *enough* in the Girls' Orphan House to take in bread (we give the bread to the children on the third day after it is baked); but before the baker came, a lady called who had had some needlework done by the children, and paid 3s. 11d., and thus the matron was able to take in bread as usual. I found this morning 2s. in the box in my house, our extremity having led me to look into it. One of the labourers gave 13s. This 15s. was divided amongst the three matrons. Thanks to the Lord, there is all that is needed for today and tomorrow.

September 30th. We are not only poor as regards the Orphan fund, but also the funds for the other objects bring us again and again to the Lord for fresh supplies. Today, when we had not a single penny in hand, £5 was given for the other objects.

October 2nd. Tuesday evening. The Lord's holy name be praised! He hath dealt most bountifully with us during the last three days! The day before yesterday £5 came in for the Orphans. Of this I gave to each house 10s., which supplied them *before the provisions were consumed.* Oh! How kind is the Lord. Always, before there has been actual want, He has sent help. Yesterday came in £1 10s. more. This £1 10s., with 4s. 2d. in hand, was divided for present necessities. Thus the expenses of yesterday, for housekeeping, were defrayed. The Lord helped me also to pay yesterday the £19 10s. for the rent. The means for it were thus obtained. One of the labourers had received through his family £10, and £5 besides from a sister in the Lord; also some other money. Of this he gave £16, which, with the £3 10s. that was left of the above mentioned £5, which came in the day before yesterday, made up £19 10s., the sum which was needed. —This day we were again greatly reduced.

There was no money in hand to take in bread as usual, for the Boys' and Infants' Orphan Houses, but again the Lord helped. A sister who had arrived this afternoon from Swansea brought £1 7s., and one of the labourers sold an article, by means of which he was able to give £1 13s. Thus we had £3—£1 for each house, and could buy bread before the day was over. Hitherto we have lacked nothing!

October 6th. The Lord has most kindly helped us. It came to my mind that there were some new blankets in the Orphan Houses, which had been given some time since, but which are not needed, and might therefore be sold. I was confirmed in this by finding that moths had got into one pair. I therefore sold ten pairs, having a good opportunity to do so. Thus the Lord not only supplied again our present need for the three houses, but I was also able to put by the rent for this week and the next, acting out the light which He had given us this day week. There came in 9s. 6d., besides £7 for the blankets. The School fund, also, was again completely exhausted, when today and yesterday came in so much, that not only the weekly salaries could be paid today, but also above £1 could be put by for rent.

October 9th. Through the last mentioned supplies for the Orphans we were helped up to this day; but today we were brought lower than ever. The provisions would have lasted out only today, and the money for milk in one of the houses could only be made up by one of the labourers selling one of his books. The matron in the Boys' Orphan House had this morning two shillings left. When in doubt whether to buy bread with it, or more meat, to make up the dinner with the meat which she had in the house, the baker called, and left three quartern of bread as a present. In this great need, some money having been given to one of the labourers, he gave £2 of it, by which we were able to buy meat, bread, and other provisions. Nevertheless, even this day, low as we had been brought before this £2 was given, there had been all in the houses that was needed.

October 10th. The Lord had sent in so much since yesterday afternoon, that we were able at our meeting this morning to divide £2 0s. 2d. between the three matrons, whereby we are helped through this day. But now the coals in the Infants' Orphan House are out, and nearly so in the other two houses. On this account we have asked the Lord for fresh supplies.

October 11th. The *"Father of the fatherless"* has again shown His care over us. An Orphan from Devonshire arrived last evening. With her was sent £2 5s. 6d. The sister who brought her gave also a silver teapot, sugar basin, and cream-jug, having found true riches in Christ. There was also in the boxes 9s. One of the labourers paid for a ton of coals. We obtained £16 16s. for the silver articles. Thus we were helped through the heavy expenses of the following days.

October 16th. The day commenced with mercies. I was looking up to the Lord for help early this morning, when, almost immediately afterwards, brother T. came, and brought two silver tablespoons and six teaspoons, which had been left anonymously, yesterday afternoon at the Girls' Orphan House. This afternoon I received £12 from Staffordshire. On the seal of the letter which enclosed the money was "Ebenezer." How true in our case! Surely this instance is a fresh "Ebenezer" to us; for hitherto the Lord has helped us.

October 27th. Saturday. This day we have been again mercifully helped, though our need has been almost greater than ever. But, thanks to our adorable Lord! This day also we have not been confounded; for there was 6s. in the box at the Infants' Orphan House, and 6s. came in for things which had been given to be sold. To this one of the labourers added 18s. By means of this £1 10s. we have been able to meet all pressing demands, and to procure provisions for today and tomorrow.

October 30th. This evening a sister gave me £20, ten of which were for the Orphans, and ten for the other objects. Thus we are helped for this week.

November 4th. Lord's day. There was given, by a stranger, last Wednesday evening, at Bethesda Chapel, to one of the sisters, a sovereign for the Orphans, which I received today. Thus the Lord has again begun the week with mercy, and His love surely will help us through it, though again many pounds will be needed.

November 7th. The funds are now again completely exhausted. Today I divided £1 3s. 8d. which had come in yesterday; thus the necessary wants were supplied. The Lord be praised who has helped us hitherto!

November 13th. This morning our want was again great. I have £20 in hand which has been put by for rent, but, for the Lord's honour, I would not take of it. Nothing had come in, and the labourers had scarcely anything to give. I went, however, to the Orphan Houses, to pray with my fellow-labourers, and, if it might be, to comfort them, and see what could be done. When I came there, I found that 19s. 6d. had come in this morning. On enquiry, I heard that only 2s. 6d. more was needed to carry us through the day. This one of the labourers was able to add. Thus the Lord has again helped us out of our difficulty. One of the labourers gave some things which he could do without, and another gave a workbox to be sold for the Orphans. Before this day has come to an end, the Lord has sent in £1 2s. 4d. more, so that we have also a little for tomorrow.

November 17th. Today above £3 was needed, and as only 15s. 6d. had come in, we found it needful to determine to dispose of a few articles of furniture which we conveniently could do without. One of the labourers gave a good watch to be sold, which she had bought some months since, there being then no timepiece in one of the houses. In consideration of these articles to be sold, I took, for the present necessities of the Orphans, £2 10s. of the money which had been put by for the rent, to be replaced when these articles could be sold at a suitable opportunity. Thus we were helped to the close of one more week.

November 20th. Today our need was exceedingly great, but the Lord's help was great also. I went to meet with the brethren and sisters as usual. I found that £1 would be needed to supply the necessities of today, but 3s. only had come in. Just when we were going to pray, one of the labourers came in, who after prayer, gave 10s. Whilst we were praying, another labourer came in, who had received £1. Thus we had £1 13s.; even more, therefore, than was absolutely needed.

November 21st. Never were we so reduced in funds as today. There was not a single half-penny in hand between the matrons of the three houses. Nevertheless there was a good dinner, and, by managing so as to help one another with bread, etc., there was a prospect of getting over this day also; but for none of the houses had we the prospect of being able to take in bread. When I left the brethren and sisters at one o'clock, after prayer, I told them that we must wait for help, and see how the Lord would deliver us at this time. I was sure of help, but we were indeed straitened. When I got to Kingsdown, I felt that I needed more exercise, being very cold; therefore I went not the nearest way home, but round by Clarence Place. About twenty yards from my house, I met a brother who walked back with me, and after a little conversation gave me £10 to be handed over to the brethren, the deacons, towards providing the poor saints with coals, blankets and warm clothing; also £5 for the Orphans, and £5 for the other Objects of the Scriptural Knowledge Institution. The brother had called twice while I was gone to the Orphan Houses, and had I now been *one half minute* later, I should have missed him. But the Lord knew our need, and therefore allowed me to meet him. I sent off the £5 immediately to the matrons.

November 24th. This again has been a very remarkable day. We had as little in hand this morning as at any time, and yet several pounds were needed. But *"God, who is rich in mercy,"* and whose Word so positively declares that none who trust in Him shall be confounded, has helped us through this day also. While I was in prayer about ten in the morning respecting the funds, I was informed that a gentleman had called to see me. He came to inform me that a lady had ordered three sacks of potatoes to be sent to the Orphan Houses. Never could they have come more seasonably. This was an encouragement to me to continue to expect help. When I came to the prayer meeting about twelve o'clock, I heard that 2s. had come in, also £1 for a guitar which had been given for sale. The payment for this guitar had been expected for many weeks. It had been mentioned among us repeatedly, that it might come just at a time when we most needed it: and oh! How true. Also the watch which had been given was sold for £2 10s....

November 28th. This is, perhaps, of all days the most remarkable as yet, so far as regards the funds. When I was in prayer this morning respecting them, I was enabled firmly to believe that the Lord would send help, though all seemed dark as to natural appearances. At twelve o'clock I met as usual with the brethren and sisters for prayer. There had come in only 1s., which was left last evening anonymously at the Infants' Orphan House, and which, except 2d., had already been spent, on account of the great need. I heard also that an individual had gratuitously cleaned the timepiece in the Infants' Orphan House, and had offered to keep the timepieces in the three houses in repair. Thus the Lord gave even in this a little encouragement, and a proof that He is still mindful of us. On enquiry I found that there was everything needful for the dinner in all the three houses; but neither in the Infants' nor Boys' Orphan Houses was there bread enough for tea, nor money to buy milk. Lower we had never been, and, perhaps never so low. We gave ourselves now unitedly to prayer, laying the case in simplicity before the Lord. Whilst in prayer there was a knock at the door, and one of the sisters went out. After the two brethren who labour in the Orphan Houses and I had prayed aloud, we continued for a while silently in prayer. As to myself, I was lifting up my heart to the Lord to make a way for our escape, and in order to know if there were any other thing which I could do with a good conscience, besides waiting on Him, so that we might have food for the children. At last we rose from our knees. I said, "God will surely send help." The words had not quite passed from my lips, when I perceived a letter lying on the table, which had been brought whilst we were in prayer. It was from my wife, containing another letter from a brother with £10 for the Orphans. The evening before last I was asked by a brother whether the balance in hand for the Orphans would be as great this time, when the accounts would be made up, as the last time. My answer was, that it would be as great as the Lord pleased. The next morning this brother was moved to remember the Orphans, and to send today £10, which arrived soon after I had left my house, and which on account of our need was forwarded immediately to me. Thus I was enabled to give £6 10s. for housekeeping, and to put by £3 10s. for rent.

November 29th. The Lord has greatly blessed our meetings for prayer. In the evening I received £50, which was sent from Suffolk by a sister who had often expressed how gladly she would contribute more largely to the work which is in our hands, had she the means, and who just now, in this our time of need, has obtained the means to carry out the desire of her heart. I rejoice in the last donation particularly, not because of the largeness of the sum, but because it enables me to pay my brethren and sisters in the Orphan Houses the salary which is due to them. For though they are willing to labour without any remuneration, nevertheless *"the labourer is worthy of his reward."* This donation also proves that the Lord is willing even now, as formerly, to send large sums. But I expect still larger. The same sister who sent the £50 for the Orphans, sent, at the same time, £30 to be divided between brother Craik and me for our personal expenses. How abundantly does the Lord care for us! Truly we serve a kind Master!

December 6th. This day our need was again as great as ever, but the deliverance of the Lord was also as manifest as ever. This afternoon I received £100 from a sister; £50 for the Orphans, and £50 for the School, Bible, and Missionary Fund. This same sister, who earns her bread with her own hands, had given, on October 5th, 1837, £50 towards the Boys' Orphan House, and gave for the necessities of the poor saints, in August, 1838, £100 more; for she had been made willing to act out those precious exhortations:

"Having food and raiment let us be therewith content." "Sell that ye have, and give alms; provide yourselves bags which wax not old, a treasure in the heavens that faileth not, where no thief approacheth, neither moth corrupteth." "Lay not up for yourselves treasures upon earth, where moth and rust doth corrupt, and where thieves break through and steal: but lay up for yourselves treasures in heaven, where neither moth nor rust doth corrupt, and where thieves do not break through nor steal"....

December 11th, 12th, and 13th. On these three days there were public meetings, at which I gave an account of the Lord's dealings with us in reference to the Orphan Houses, and the other Objects of the Scriptural Knowledge Institution. As the work, and particularly that of the Orphan Houses, was begun for the benefit of the Church at large, it appeared well to us, that from time to time it should be publicly stated how the Lord had dealt with us; and as the third year had been completed, this seemed to be a suitable time for having these meetings.

Should any one suppose, in reading the plain details of the trials through which we passed during the four months previous to December 9th, 1838, respecting the Orphan Houses, that I have been disappointed as regards my expectations, as far as the funds are concerned: my answer is, that the reverse is the case. For straits were expected. Long before the trials came I had more than once stated publicly, that answers to prayer in the time of need—the manifestation of the hand of God, stretched out for our help—was just the very end for which the Institution was established.

I further state that the Orphans have never lacked anything. Had I had thousands of pounds in hand, they would have fared no better than they have; for they have always had good nourishing food, the necessary articles of clothing, etc.

Large Gifts from Unlikely Sources

These last two entries have the purpose of demonstrating that God not only has the power to deliver on a daily, even hourly basis with small gifts, but He also has the power to send great gifts, and from the most unlikely sources.

–Large Donation from a Poor Seamstress (1835)

December 18th. This afternoon a brother brought from a sister, a counterpane, a flat iron stand, eight cups and saucers, a sugar basin, a milk jug, a tea cup, sixteen thimbles, five knives and forks, six dessert spoons, twelve tea spoons, four combs, and two little graters; from another friend a flat iron and a cup and saucer. At the same time he brought £100 from a sister. It has since pleased the Lord to take to Himself the donor of this £100, and I therefore give further account of the donation and the donor, as the particulars respecting both, with God's blessing, may tend to edification. Indeed, I confess that I am delighted to be at liberty, in consequence of the death of the donor, to give the following short narrative, which, during her lifetime, I should not have considered it wise to publish. A.L., the donor, was known to me almost from the beginning of my coming to Bristol in 1832. She earned her bread by needlework, by which she gained from 2s. to 5s. per week; the average, I suppose, was not more than about 3s. 6d., as she was weak in body. But this dear, humble sister was content with her small earnings, and I do not remember ever to have heard her utter a word of complaint on account of earning so little. Some time before I had been led to establish an Orphan House, her father had died, through which event she had come into the possession of £480, which sum had been left to her (and the same amount to her brother and two sisters) by her grandmother, but of which her father had had the interest during his lifetime. The father, who had been much given to drink, died in debt, which debts the children wished to pay; but the rest, besides A. L., did not like to pay the full amount, and offered to the creditors 5s. in the pound, which they gladly accepted, as they had not the least legal claim upon the children. After the debts had been paid according to this agreement, A. L. said to herself, "However sinful my father may have been, yet he was my father, and as I have the means of paying his debts to the full amount, I ought, as a believing child, to do so, seeing that my brother and sisters will not do it."

She then went to all the creditors secretly, and paid the full amount of the debts, which took £40 more of her money, besides her share which she had given before. Her brother and two sisters now gave £50 each of their property to their mother; but A. L. said to herself: "I am a child of God, surely I ought to give my mother twice as much as my brother and sisters." She, therefore, gave her mother £100. Shortly after this she sent me the £100 towards the Orphan House. I was not a little surprised when I received this money from her, for I had always known her as a poor girl, and I had never heard anything about her having come into the possession of this money, and her dress had never given me the least indication of an alteration in her circumstances. Before, however, accepting this money from her, I had a long conversation with her, in which I sought to probe her as to her motives, and in which I sought to ascertain whether, as I had feared, she might have given this money in the feeling of the moment, without having counted the cost. I was the more particular, because, if the money were given, without its being given from Scriptural motives, and there should be regret afterwards, the name of the Lord would be dishonoured.

But I had not conversed long with this beloved sister, before I found that she was, in this particular, a quiet, calm, considerate follower of the Lord Jesus, and one who desired, in spite of what human reason might say, to act according to the words of our Lord: *"Lay not up for yourselves treasures upon earth"* (Matthew 6:19). *"Sell that ye have and give alms"* (Luke 12:33). When I remonstrated with her, in order that I might see whether she had counted the cost, she said to me: "The Lord Jesus has given His *last* drop of blood for me, and should I not give Him this £100?" She likewise said: "Rather than the Orphan House should not be established, I will give all the money I have." When I saw that she had weighed the matter according to the Word of God, and that she had counted the cost, I could not but take the money, and admire the way which the Lord took, to use this poor, sickly sister as an instrument, in so considerable a measure, for helping, at its very commencement, this work, which I had set about solely in dependence upon the living God.

At that time, she would also have me take £5 for the poor saints in communion with us. I mention here particularly, that this dear sister kept all these things to herself, and did them as much as possible in secret; and during her lifetime, I suppose, not six brethren and sisters among us knew that she had ever possessed £480, or that she had given £100 towards the Orphan House. But this is not all. Some time after this £100 had been given by her, brother C—r (who was then labouring as a City Missionary in connection with the Scriptural Knowledge Institution, and who about that very time happened to visit from house to house in that part of the city where A. L. lived) told me that he had met with many cases in which she had given, to one poor woman a bedstead, to another some bedding, to another some clothes, to another food; and thus instance upon instance of acts of love, on the part of our dear sister, had come before him. I relate one instance more.

August 4th, 1836, seven months and a half after she had given the £100, she came one morning to me and said: "Last evening I felt myself particularly stirred up to pray about the funds of the Scriptural Knowledge Institution; but whilst praying I thought, *what good is it for me to pray for means, if I do not give when I have the means*, and I have therefore brought you this £5." As I had reason to believe that by this time by far the greater part of her money was gone, I again had a good deal of conversation with her, to see whether she really did count the cost, and whether this donation also was given unto the Lord, or from momentary excitement, in which case it was better not to give the money. However, she was at this time also steadfast, grounded upon the Word of God, and evidently constrained by the love of Christ; and all the effect my conversation had upon her was, that she said: "You must take five shillings in addition to the £5, as a proof that I give the £5 cheerfully." Four things are specially to be noticed about this beloved sister, with reference to all this period of her earthly pilgrimage: (1) She did all these things in secret, avoiding to the utmost all show about them, and thus proved that she did not desire the praise of man. (2) She remained, as before, of a humble and lowly mind, and she proved thus, that she had done what she did unto the Lord, and not unto man. (3) Her dress remained, during all the time that she had this comparative abundance, the same as before. It was clean, yet as simple and inexpensive as it was at the time when all her income had consisted of 3s. 6d., or at most 5s., per week. There was not the least difference as to her lodging, dress, manner of life, etc. She remained in every way the poor handmaid of the Lord, as to all outward appearance. (4) But that which is as lovely as the rest, she continued working at her needle all this time. She earned her 2s. 6d., or 3s., or a little more, a week, as before; whilst she gave away the money in sovereigns or five-pound notes.

At last all her money was gone, and that some years before she fell asleep; and as her bodily health never had been good, as long as I had known her, and was now much worse, she found herself peculiarly dependent upon the Lord, who never forsook her up to the last moment of her earthly course. The very commencement of her life of simple dependence upon the Lord, was such as greatly to encourage her. She related the facts to me as I give them here. When she was completely without money, and when her little stock of tea and butter was also gone, two sisters in the Lord called on her. After they had been a little while with her, they told her that they had come to take tea with her. She said to herself, I should not at all mind going without my tea, but this is a great trial, that I have nothing to set before these sisters; and she gave them therefore to understand that their staying to tea would not be convenient at that time. The sisters, however, I suppose, not understanding the hint, remained, and presently brought out of a basket tea, sugar, butter and bread, and thus there was all that was requisite for the tea, and the remainder of the provisions was left for her. She told me that at that time she was not accustomed to trials of faith, as she afterwards was.

Her body became weaker and weaker, in consequence of which she was able to work very little for many months before she died; but the Lord supplied her with all she needed, though she never asked for anything. For instance, a sister in communion with us sent her for many months all the bread she used. Her mouth was full of thanksgiving, even in the midst of the greatest bodily sufferings. She fell asleep in Jesus in January, 1844. I have related these facts because they tend to the praise of the Lord, and may be instrumental in stirring up other children of God to follow this dear departed sister in so far as she followed the Lord Jesus; but, in particular, that I may show in what remarkable ways the Lord proved, from the very beginning, that the Orphan House was His and not mine.

–Gift of Eight Thousand One Hundred Pounds (1853)

January 4th. Day by day I have now been waiting upon God for means for the Building Fund for more than nineteen months, and almost daily I have received something in answer to prayer. These donations have been, for the most part, small, in comparison with the amount which will be required for the completion of this object; nevertheless they have shown that the Lord, for the sake of His dear Son, listens to my supplications and to those of my fellow labourers and helpers in the work; and they have been precious encouragements to me to continue to wait upon God. I have been for many months assured that the Lord, in His own time, would give larger sums for this work; and for this I have been more and more earnestly entreating Him, during the last months. Now at last He has abundantly refreshed my spirit, and answered my request. I received today the promise, that, *as the joint donation of several Christians*, there should be paid to me a donation of eight thousand and one hundred pounds for the work of the Lord in my hands. Of this sum I purpose to take £6,000 for the Building Fund.

See how precious it is to wait upon God! See how those who do so, are not confounded! Their faith and patience may long and sharply be tried; but in the end it will most assuredly be seen, that those who honour God He will honour, and will not suffer them to be put to shame. The largeness of the donation, whilst it exceedingly refreshed my spirit, did not in the least surprise me; *for I expect GREAT things from God.*

March 14th. From Scotland £200, of which the donor kindly wished me to give £10 to Mr. Craik, to take £10 for my own personal expenses, and to use the £180 as most needed. I took, therefore, £100 for the Building Fund.

March 29th. For nearly three months the Lord has been pleased to exercise my patience by the comparatively small amount of means which has come in. Now, this evening, when I came home, I found that £300 had come in. This is a great refreshment to my spirit. As the amount is left to my disposal as may be most needed, I have taken one half of it for the Building Fund.

May 14th. Received £260, of which I took £100 for the Building Fund.

June 28th. From Wakefield £40, with £5 for Mr. Craik, and £5 for my own personal expenses. Also £220 from the West of England, of which the donor kindly wishes me to take £20 for my own private expenses, and to use the £200 as might be most needed. I have taken, therefore, £100 for the Building Fund.

July 14th. Received £541 10s., which being left to me as most needed, I took £341 10s. for the Building Fund.

July 15th. Received £110 from one who counts it an honour to have this sum to lay down at the feet of the Lord Jesus. I took of this amount £60 for the Building Fund.

I cannot help remarking here, that the Lord has used some of the most unlikely persons during the past twenty-two years, in providing me with means for His service. So it was particularly in the case of this brother in the Lord, from whom I received the last-mentioned donation of £110. I had not the least natural expectation of receiving this sum, when this brother, sitting before me at the New Orphan House, took out of his pocket a packet of Bank Notes, and gave to me this amount, reserving to himself, as his whole property *in this world*, a smaller sum than he gave to me, because of his joy in the Lord, and because of his being able to enter into the reality of his possessions *in the world to come*. I delight in dwelling upon such an instance, because: (1) It shows that there is grace, much grace, to be found among the saints even now; (2) It shows the variety of instrumentality which the Lord is pleased to employ, in supplying me with means for His service; and (3) Because it so manifestly proves that we do not wait upon Him in vain, when we make known our requests to Him for means.

December 31st. This is the last day of another year. Two years and a half I have now been day by day seeking the Lord's help in prayer for this object. He has also been pleased to give us many proofs that He is remembering our requests....

– VI –

REASONS FOR DESIRING TO ESTABLISH
AN ORPHAN HOUSE.

I had constantly cases brought before me, which proved that one of the special things which the children of God needed in our day, was, to have their faith strengthened. I longed to have something to point to, as a visual proof, that our God and Father is the same faithful God as ever He was; as willing as ever to prove Himself to be the LIVING God, in our day as formerly, to all who put their trust in Him. Sometimes I found children of God tried in mind by the prospect of old age, when they might be unable to work any longer, and therefore were harassed by the fear of having to go into the poor house.

If in such a case I pointed out to them, how their Heavenly Father has always helped those who put their trust in Him, though they might not always say that times have changed; yet it was evident enough, that God was not looked upon by them as the LIVING God. My Spirit was ofttimes bowed down by this, and I longed to set something before the children of God, whereby they might see, that He does not forsake, even in our day, those who rely upon Him. Also I longed to be instrumental in strengthening their faith, by giving them not only instances from the Word of God, of His willingness and ability to help all those who rely upon Him, but to show them by proofs, that He is the same in our day. I well knew that the Word of God ought to be enough, and it was by grace, enough for me; but still, I considered that I ought to lend a helping hand to my brethren, if by any means, by this visible proof of the unchangeable faithfulness of the Lord I might strengthen their hands in God; for I remembered what a great blessing my own soul had received through the Lord's dealings with His servant A. H. Franke, who, in dependence upon the living God alone established an immense orphan house, which I had seen many times with my own eyes. I, therefore, judged myself bound to be the servant of the church of God, in the particular point on which I had obtained mercy: namely, in being able to take God at His word and to rely upon it.

All these exercises of my soul, which resulted from the fact that many believers, with whom I became acquainted, were harassed and distressed in mind, or brought guilt on their consciences, on account of not trusting in the Lord; were used by God to awaken in my heart the desire of setting before the church at large, and before the world, a proof that He has not in the least changed; and this seemed to me best done by the establishing of an orphan house. It needed to be something which could be seen, even by the natural eye. Now, if I, a poor man, simply by prayer and faith, obtained, without asking any individual, the means for establishing and carrying on an orphan house: there would be something which, with the Lord's blessing, might be instrumental in strengthening the faith of the children of God, besides being a testimony to the consciences of the unconverted, of the reality of the things of God. This, then, was the primary reason for establishing the orphan house. I certainly did from my heart desire to be used by God to benefit the bodies of poor children, bereaved of both parents, and seek, in other respects, with the help of God, to do them good for this life—I also particularly longed to be used by God in getting the dear orphans trained up in the fear of God—but still the first and primary object of the work was (and still is), that God might be magnified by the fact, that the orphans under my care are provided with all they need, only by prayer and faith without anyone being asked by me or my fellow-labourers, whereby it may be seen, that God is FAITHFUL STILL, and HEARS PRAYER STILL.

– VII –

EXHORTATION TO PERSEVERANCE IN PRAYER
(1863)

Thus I saw the close of another year, with reference to this part of the work. The full answer to my daily prayers was far from being realized; yet there was abundant encouragement granted by the Lord, to continue in prayer. But suppose, even, that far less had come in than was received, still, after having come to the conclusion, upon scriptural ground, and after much prayer and self-examination, as stated at full length before, I ought to have gone on without wavering, in the exercise of faith and patience concerning this object (*i.e.* the building of a new orphanage); and thus all the children of God, when once satisfied that anything which they bring before God in prayer is according to His will, ought to continue in believing, expecting, persevering prayer, until the blessing is granted. Thus am I myself now (*viz.* in 1864) waiting upon God for certain blessings, for which I have daily besought Him for 19 years and 6 months, without one day's intermission. Still the full answer is not yet given concerning the conversion of certain individuals, though, in the meantime, I have received many thousands of answers to prayer. I have also prayed daily, without intermission, for the conversion of other individuals about ten years, for others six or seven years, for others four, three, and two years, for others about eighteen months; and still the answer is not yet granted, concerning *these* persons: whilst, in the meantime, many thousands of my prayers have been answered, and also souls converted, for whom I had been praying. I lay particular stress upon this, for the benefit of a certain class of readers, who may suppose that I need only to ask God, and receive at once; or that I might pray concerning anything, and the answer would surely come. One can only expect to obtain answers to prayers which are according to the mind of God; and even then, patience and faith may be exercised for many years, even as mine are exercised, in the latter to which I have referred; and yet am I daily continuing in prayer, and expecting the answer, and so certainly expecting the answer that I have often thanked God that He will surely give it, though now for 19 years and 6 months faith and patience have thus been exercised. Be encouraged, dear Christian reader, with fresh earnestness to give yourself to prayer, if you can only be sure that you ask for things which are for the glory of God.

Yours affectionately
George Müller